COLONIAL SUNSET

The author, L.W. (Les) Johnson.

COLONIAL SUNSET
Australia and
Papua New Guinea
1970–74

L.W. JOHNSON

University of Queensland Press
ST LUCIA • LONDON • NEW YORK

© University of Queensland Press, St Lucia, Queensland 1983

Typeset by University of Queensland Press
Printed and bound by The Dominion Press–Hedges & Bell, Melbourne

Distributed in the United Kingdom, Europe, the Middle East,
Africa, and the Caribbean by Prentice-Hall International,
International Book Distributors Ltd, 66 Wood Lane End, Hemel Hempstead, Herts.,
England.

National Library of Australia
Cataloguing-in-Publication data

Johnson, L.W. (Leslie Wilson), 1916–.
    Colonial sunset.

    Includes index.
    ISBN 0 7022 1823 5.

    1. Papua New Guinea — Politics and government.
    2. Australia — Colonies — Administration.
    I. Title.

325′.394′0995

995.3
J57

Library of Congress Cataloging in Publication Data

Johnson, L.W. (Leslie Wilson), 1917–
    Colonial sunset.

    Includes index.
    1. Papua New Guinea — Politics and government — To 1975.
2. Australia — Politics and government — 1945–
3. Johnson, L.W. (Leslie Wilson), 1917–   I. Title.
DU740.75.J63   1983   995′.3   82-21875
ISBN 0-7022-1823-5

Designed by Paul Rendle

For Dulcie

CONTENTS

ILLUSTRATIONS

*Note: All photographs were provided by the former Papua New
Guinea Department of Information and Extension Services, with
the exception of the photograph on page 153, Port Moresby
becomes a city, April 1972, which is reproduced by permission
of the* Post Courier, *Port Moresby.*

PREFACE

This book contains a personal account of four years of Papua New Guinea history in which I was intimately involved. It makes no pretensions to being comprehensive. I write about the things which had the greatest impact on me, and, no doubt, I deal in an unjustifiably cursory fashion with some events of considerable importance. A large part of the supporting material which I have used in compiling the manuscript comes from personal papers accumulated by my official secretary in Papua New Guinea and despatched to me long after my departure. Those wishing to see the papers may do so in the National Archives. Readers may find tedious my propensity to quote myself — usually at some length. My justification for so doing, apart from the pride of authorship, is that such quotes have been taken from documents, or speeches, produced at the time, reflecting attitudes of that time, and have not been bowdlerized in hindsight to improve the writer's image or magnify his sagacity. I beg your tolerance for my self-indulgence.

I have terminated my account shortly after Self-Government Day because that is as far as my direct personal experience of Papua New Guinea affairs stretches.

It may have been tidier to conclude at Independence Day in September 1975, but for all practical purposes Papua New Guinea had full control of its own affairs from 1 December 1973. Papua New Guinea had come a long way in a breathlessly short space of time since the first general election for a House of Assembly in 1964.

I have everywhere referred to the language used for general communication in Papua New Guinea as "Pidgin", though now the official name is "Tok Pisin". I have used names as they were at the time about which I write; for instance, "Districts" are now "Provinces", and the "Chimbu" is now the "Simbu". Many of the principal figures have become knights — Julius Chan, Paul Lapun, Albert Maori Kiki, John Guise, Tore Lokoloko, Pita Lus, David Hay and Tei Abal among them. I use the term "we" freely throughout the book. This is intended to comprehend the Papua New Guinea Administration which, of course, carried forward the policy of the Australian Government.

It should be borne in mind that what was done by Australians, or left undone, was not the work of any one individual or even of one group. It was the result of the co-operative efforts of many. The policies which were pursued, with greater or lesser diligence, were fixed by the Australian Government, enunciated by its Minister for External Territories, who was advised by his Department. The Papua New Guinea Administration was the executive arm. However, during the period I have reviewed, there was the closest co-operation between the Department and the Administration. We, in the Administration, were deficient in skilled manpower in many fields, and relied for help upon our colleagues in Australia, help which was always freely and generously available. The Administration and the Department enjoyed a fruitful partnership. We were indebted to the Secretary to the Department,

David Hay, and to all his officers, of whom only a few can be listed here: John Greenwell and Alan Kerr, who masterminded the devolution of power; Tim Besley, whose administrative skills were an invaluable support; Gerry Gutman and Don Mentz who provided back-up for our somewhat frail resources in economic know-how.

I have made scant reference to individual expatriate public servants, many of whom spent their entire working lives in Papua New Guinea. Setting aside the usual proportion of time-servers found in any public service, they were a loyal and hard-working body, interested in their jobs and with an abiding affection for the country for which they worked. Chief among them was Tony Newman, Deputy Administrator, who, among other things, was the Administration's eyes, ears and voice in the House of Assembly. He was an official member of the House from its inception in 1964 until he retired in 1973. His parliamentary longevity was shared, in 1973, with eight elected members, one of them an expatriate public servant turned businessman, Ron Neville.

Almost in the public servant category is the wife of any administrator, for the job of Administrator has responsibilities, and the public has concomitant expectations, which could not be adequately encompassed without the active participation of a partner. I was fortunate enough to have a wife who cheerfully undertook a wide range of responsibilities and enjoyed doing so.

In Papua New Guinea a very special service was given by three expatriate officers who handled with tact and skill the induction of the National Coalition Goverment and its assumption of power — Paul Ryan, Mark Lynch and Thos Barnett. Their task was made easier by the people they dealt with; in particular by Tony Voutas, and by Michael Somare himself. Papua New Guineans are prominent enough in the text that follows, so that mention here is superfluous. We were singularly fortunate that most of the indigenous leaders were people of good sense and it was my particular good fortune to number many of them among my close personal friends.

Papua New Guinea got away to a pretty good start under the leadership of Michael Somare. He was succeeded, in the Westminster tradition, by Julius Chan who was once his deputy but, at this later date, is on the opposite side of the political fence. As I write, Papua New Guinea has just completed its fifth general election which has resulted in the return to power of Michael Somare with what appears to be a comfortable majority. His Pangu Pati is supported by the United Party, once Pangu's implacable opponent. Only two members of those who formed the first House of Assembly in 1964 remain, Pita Lus, now a knight, and presently Minister of State for Parliamentary Services, and Barry Holloway, Minister for Education. Holloway, however, has not had the continuous parliamentary service of Lus, having missed out in the 1968 election for the second House of Assembly. Lus has served in all five parliaments. To us old-timers parliament will not seem the same without those well known political veterans, Sir John Guise, Sir Tei Abal and Sir Paul Lapun.

ABBREVIATIONS

AEC	The Administrator's Executive Council
AGPS	Australian Government Publishing Service
CPC	Constitutional Planning Committee
DET	Department of External Territories
ESS	Employment Security Scheme
HAD	House of Assembly Debates
MA	Mataungan Association
MHA	Member of the House of Assembly
MRC	Multiracial Council
NBC	National Broadcasting Commission
NCG	National Coalition Government
PIR	Pacific Islands Regiment
P.N.G.	Papua New Guinea
PP	Personal Papers

1

PROLOGUE

On 5 May 1970 I was appointed Administrator of Papua New Guinea, and I took up the position some two months later, on 23 July. I was not a newcomer, as I had served in the country since February 1962. I first came to Papua New Guinea as Deputy Director of Education, and became Director of the Education Department a few months later, on the retirement of the incumbent, Geoffrey Roscoe. In 1966, when John Gunther, the Assistant Administrator, resigned to become Vice-Chancellor of the new university, I took over his job and held it until my resignation from the Papua New Guinea service on 28 April 1970.

My appointment as Administrator, and that of my predecessor, David Hay, as Secretary, Department of External Territories, in 1970, aroused some controversy and speculation at the time. The two appointments required some bureaucratic reshuffling of departmental heads in Canberra and came about primarily because of events in Papua New Guinea.

Hay had departed on leave from Papua New Guinea just before Christmas, in 1969, and I was Acting Administrator when, in late December, Gough Whitlam, then Leader of the Opposition, accompanied by a retinue of half-a-dozen or so, arrived in Port Moresby for a fortnight's tour of the country. In Australia at the time, the Labor Party was mounting a strong challenge to the coalition government led by John Gorton, and Whitlam clearly came to Papua New Guinea looking for issues. He had already decided that self-government or independence for Papua New Guinea was an issue on which the Australian Government was vulnerable, as was the responsible Minister, C.E. Barnes, a senior and conservative member of the Country Party. The Prime Minister, John Gorton, had not evinced much interest in Papua New Guinea affairs, except to comment on the magnitude of Australian aid to Papua New Guinea, associated with the comment "they can become self-governing and independent as soon as a method is devised".[1] Whitlam, on the other hand, had always shown a lively interest in Papua New Guinea, having visited it several times and having, on occasion, made thoughtful contributions to debates on its affairs. Kim Beazley, a member of the group accompanying him on this occasion, had always been the best-informed member of Parliament on Papua New Guinea, apart from Paul Hasluck.

At any rate, Whitlam set out to exploit both the conservatism of the Australian Government towards constitutional advancement for Papua New Guinea, and the lack of interest of the Prime Minister and most of his colleagues in Papua New Guinea affairs. The early weeks of January 1970 were sparse ones for news, Papua New Guinea was a new scene for Australian readers, and Whitlam used the situation with skill. Papua New Guinea came out of the bottom drawer of Australian politics and immediately became a matter of political confrontation. In addition, Whitlam did not spare local residents, whether they were Papuan New Guinean or Australian. At a public meeting in

Hanuabada, a large Port Moresby village, he called the village leaders, who were also prominent national politicians, "Uncle Toms". Whitlam, on his way from Hanuabada to eat with my wife and me, was preceded by an infuriated telephone call from one of those despised leaders, Oala Oala Rarua, the Minister for the Treasury, who in no sense regarded himself as a conservative, urging me to despatch "that bastard" back to Canberra forthwith.

On Whitlam's departure, rather later than Oala Rarua had suggested, he issued a statement clearly outlining Labor's policy towards Papua New Guinea. He said that a decision on self-government and independence was not solely a decision for Papua New Guinea but one which was also the responsibility of the Australian parliament, and prophetically continued

> an Australian election must be held by the end of 1972 at the latest . . . It is our belief that a Labor Government will emerge from those elections . . . New Guineans will have home rule as soon as a Labor Government can make the necessary arrangements with the House of Assembly which will also be elected in 1972.
>
> . . . [Papuan New Guinea] is not unique in its economy, in the difference of economic standards between sections of the country, its educational or social standards, its need for economic aid from abroad, its need for advisers, the diversity of local customs, or even the multiplicity of its languages . . . None of these problems require colonial rule for their solution or easing . . . An outside administration cannot teach or impose unity. It can by errors unite a people against it. This is the very situation which Australians at home will not permit.[2]

The publicity and the ensuing controversy proved an embarrassment for the Australian Government which was heightened as, at this time I, perforce, had to announce my resignation from the Papua New Guinea service. As this was taken as further evidence that all was not well with the Australian Administration of Papua New Guinea, my decision to resign, and the timing of it, require some explanation, for my motives have been misconstrued. It has been said, variously, that my resignation was due to my dissatisfaction with the Australian Government policies towards Papua New Guinea, that I could no longer put up with the heavy controlling hand of the Department of External Territories; and that I disagreed with David Hay's administration. I guess there is an element of truth in some of these suppositions, particularly those concerning the frustrations induced by the constantly strained relations between External Territories and the Administration of Papua New Guinea, because of the Secretary of the Department's attempt to control every aspect of Papua New Guinea affairs in the name of his Minister. My most difficult experiences were in the development and management of Papua New Guinea's works programme, where even minor items had to be referred to Canberra for approval, but more particularly in the House of Assembly where, as Senior Official Member, I was harassed to produce conformity with the Department's views of Papua New Guinea affairs. This seemed to me to be a direct negation of the purpose of the House of Assembly, where one should have been seeking to meet, at least halfway, the wishes of the elected representatives of the people of Papua New Guinea. I expect that my irritations were enhanced by the knowledge that the Secretary, George Warwick Smith, had opposed my earlier appointment as Assistant Administrator. After my resignation had been announced, he confirmed his opinion of me in criticism of the decision of the Constitutional Committee of the House of Assembly to retain me as an adviser after my resignation from the Papua New Guinea service. However, I enjoyed an amicable relationship with David Hay; in the course of close association over seven years, we always got on pretty well.

By the middle of 1969 I had been in Papua New Guinea more than seven years. I was then fifty-three years of age, and that fact, allied with my general dissatisfaction with External Territories overlordship, helped me to decide that it was time to go if any interesting Australian-based job turned up. It might be noted that my appointment as Assistant Administrator was to conclude in mid–1971 and, given my relationship with External Territories and possible political advances in Papua New Guinea, an extension of employment might be unlikely. It seemed better to look for a job as a currently-employed senior public servant of fifty-three than as a discarded one of fifty-five. In this situation, I accepted the position of Principal of the newly-created Tasmanian College of Advanced Education (T.C.A.E.) in late 1969, but I requested a deferment of the announcement until early January 1970, promising to take up the appointment in May 1970.

The Whitlam furore was at its height, when my resignation and my Tasmanian appointment were announced, though the date for the announcement had been fixed with the Council for the T.C.A.E. long before Whitlam's visit. It was said that my timing was deliberately intended to embarrass the Australian Government, but this was certainly not so. I was pressed to give my reasons for resignation, which I did, in a letter to the local Port Moresby newspaper, the *Post Courier*. In the letter I stated that I was not resigning because of dissatisfaction but because I wanted to assure my future, as my five-year appointment as Assistant Administrator was to conclude shortly.

In Canberra, the Whitlam visit and my own resignation put the Government under some pressure to mend its colonial image, to improve the relationship between External Territories and the Administration of Papua New Guinea, and to pull some of the rug from under Whitlam's feet by projecting a progressive attitude, but how to do it was difficult to decide. As a replacement of the Country Party Minister for External Territories could not be contemplated, a reshuffle of the top bureaucracy associated with devolution of powers to Papua New Guinea seemed to be the best solution to the problem.

In February 1970 the P.N.G. House of Assembly's Select Committee on Constitutional Development visited Canberra for discussions on future political development with Australian Ministers and officials. One of the meetings was with the Prime Minister. To Gorton the committee expressed their concern at my resignation and asked for his intervention. Other similar representations had been made by groups of House of Assembly members and other residents of Papua New Guinea. Shortly afterwards, the Administrator, David Hay, visited Canberra and spoke with the Prime Minister, and it was about this time that Gorton decided that the answer to his political problem was to move Warwick Smith from External Territories. Hay returned to Port Moresby in some excitement, and asked my reaction to an appointment as Deputy Administrator in residence, while he filled the dual position of Secretary for External Territories and Administrator, but based permanently in Canberra with regular visits to Papua New Guinea. Without too much cogitation, I told him that I would accept an appointment as Administrator but none other. There the matter rested.

However, progress continued in Canberra. The possible moves were becoming clear, but whether or not a decision to implement them would be made was unresolved. It was known that Smith would not be too reluctant to accept a move to Interior and that Kingsland of Interior would look kindly on a transfer to Repatriation to replace the retiring incumbent, Sir Frederick Chilton.

My retirement from the Papua New Guinea service was scheduled for 28 April 1970, and I made it clear that if I was offered the job of Administrator I would expect the personal intervention of the Prime Minister with my prospective Tasmanian employers, as I had formally accepted the offer of a post and could not withdraw honourably without his intervention. I further said that if I actually reached Hobart and took up the new position I would feel obliged to stay. As far as I was concerned the whole deal had to be completed before 5 May and, of course, preferably before 28 April, the day I was to leave Papua New Guinea.

Hay was in fairly constant contact with Canberra, but Gorton, both the architect and the builder of the situation, had other preoccupations; 27 April passed without any finality and my wife and I left the following day for a week in Melbourne and a winter wardrobe. It still seemed likely that changes were intended, but I was firm in my intention not to return to Papua New Guinea once I had begun my new job in Hobart. But apparently my departure activated the Canberra machine. The day after we arrived in Melbourne, I received an urgent call from Barnes, Minister for External Territories, telling me that great changes were in train, and offering me the position of Administrator. The news came just in time for me to check my wife's fixed intention to buy a fur coat. Without undue reluctance I told Barnes that I would accept the post if the Prime Minister got me off the Tasmanian hook, which he did by calling Bethune, the Tasmanian Premier. The appointment of Hay as Secretary, External Territories and my appointment as Administrator, Papua New Guinea were made public on 5 May, the day I was to have taken up the Tasmanian appointment. As earlier indicated, Smith went to Interior and Kingsland to Repatriation.

The appointments relieved some of the pressure on the Prime Minister as far as Papua New Guinea affairs were concerned, and set up a relationship between the Department and the Administration which ensured greater co-operation than before. It also brought the matter of increased internal responsibility in Papua New Guinea to the fore and paved the way for the Prime Minister's visit to Papua New Guinea in mid-year to announce the grant of extensive additional powers to Ministers in Papua New Guinea.

Whitlam's claim to be the catalyst in the ensuing rapid movement to self-government in Papua New Guinea is undeniably correct.

NOTES

1. Reported in "This Week" H.S.V. 7 interview, 4 July 1969.
2. Statement by the Leader of the Opposition, E.G. Whitlam, Port Moresby, 12 January 1970, copy among PP.

2

THE INHERITANCE

The repercussions from the Whitlam visit induced changes in Canberra attitudes towards Papua New Guinea almost immediately. In the first week in 1970 Papua New Guinea's Select Committee on Constitutional Development was, as previously mentioned, in Canberra. Barnes told the Committee that Ministerial Members of Papua New Guinea[1] were to be given more responsibilities and that the Australian Government would not wait on the Committee's report before giving more powers to the Administrator's Executive Council (AEC). The AEC was presided over by the Administrator and comprised seven Ministerial Members, three official members of the House of Assembly and one other member of the House appointed at the discretion of the Administrator. The Prime Minister told the Select Committee "we are actually talking about . . . quick steps towards the transfer of authority to the Administrator, to the Administrator's Executive Council and to Ministerial Members, leading to a lessening of need to refer matters to Canberra for decision."[2] Hay added to the pressure, saying, in a letter to the Minister, "I am now convinced that only an early transfer of some real power . . . can secure the sense of involvement and responsibility."[3]

The concern of the Prime Minister was further increased by the adverse publicity arising from events in the Gazelle Peninsula on the island of New Britain, where a large force of riot police was needed to contain threatened violence from members of the Mataungan Association,[4] and by news of police action in Bougainville to enforce the resumption of land owned by Papua New Guineans for the development of a town for the workers on the large copper mine then being established. Changes of substance were obviously necessary for Australian political purposes, irrespective of pressures in Papua New Guinea.

By May 1970 the Department of External Territories had been spurred into action to produce a paper — "Implications of the early achievement of self-government". The submission made these points: "In the past years the Government's expressed policy of making changes when the people want them has tended to become synonymous with moving at the pace of the slowest. In 1972 there would be insufficient Papua New Guineans for self-government. Self-government is thus unlikely to have support of the majority of the people."[5] Hay responded to the draft — "I strongly support the general thesis that the area of final decision-making [in P.N.G.] . . . should be enlarged . . . in general the Commonwealth should lean towards rather than against the early achievement of self-government."[6]

The whole process of alteration of attitudes and policies culminated in a five-day visit made to Papua New Guinea in July by Prime Minister Gorton. In Rabaul, he was received by a hostile crowd of upwards of 10,000 supporters of the Mataungan Association. This influenced the Prime Minister's later decision to make the Pacific Islands Regiment available to assist the police in the maintenance of order, if required. There was some fear that violence might erupt during the

Prime Minister's address to the menacing crowd in Rabaul and members of his party carried concealed arms while a helicopter was in readiness to evacuate the Prime Minister if necessary. Fortunately the confrontation was confined to verbal pyrotechnics. Gorton also visited Bougainville, and got little joy there either. As a response to secession talk by the Bougainvilleans, he made reference to regionalization, a theme later developed to immodest proportions by ambitious provincial politicians.

However, the Prime Minister's principal purpose was to make a dramatic step forwards in the approach to self-government. He wasted no time about it, and made his major policy speech at a dinner on 6 July, the day after his arrival in Papua New Guinea. Key points in his statement were:

> We believe that the time has come when less should be referred to Canberra for decision and more should be retained for decision by the Administrator's Executive Council and the Ministerial Members . . . And we also propose that the Parliament of Australia will not exercise its veto power in relation to Ordinances if those Ordinances affect the actual responsibilities handed over to Ministerial Members.[7]

The Prime Minister listed the areas for local decision, which excluded only the judiciary, the enforcement of law and order, external affairs, external trade and large scale development projects. He emphasized the continuation of Australia's support and outlined a new method of providing financial assistance which effectively provided for local responsibility for the expenditure of funds raised within Papua New Guinea. Thus a very large measure of responsibility was placed (dumped, some would say) in local hands, if they chose to use it, and gave the Chairman of the AEC, shortly to be myself, a rather precarious balancing act in the nature and extent of the influence he could, or should, exercise over the Council and over Ministerial Members.

Barnes followed the Prime Minister, and outlined some of the practical steps to be taken to implement the announcement. Effectively the Commonwealth *Papua and New Guinea Act* 1949 was the constitution of Papua New Guinea and in normal circumstances an amendment to the Act would be required to effect changes in the disposition of powers and responsibilities. But earlier amendments (in May 1968) had enabled proclamations of the Governor-General's instructions in the *Commonwealth of Australia Gazette* to be used as a direct means of transferring powers and functions under sections 15 and 25 of the Act without awaiting time-consuming amendments to the Act itself. This procedure had the additional advantage, if needed, that instructions could be withdrawn with equal facility should the situation require it. The brief for the Administrator was contained in Section 15 of the amended Act (*Papua and New Guinea Act* 1949–68);

> The Administrator shall exercise and perform all powers that belong to his office in accordance with the tenor of his commission and in accordance with such instructions as are given to him by the Governor-General.

Section 25 (2) provided that:

> Powers, functions and duties in relation to the Government of the Territory shall not be imposed on the holder of a Ministerial Office in his capacity as the holder of such an office, but this sub-section does not operate so as to prevent the delegation to the holder of a ministerial office of powers or functions under an ordinance.[8]

The purpose of these amendments was to short-circuit the process of extending additional powers to Papuan New Guinean Ministers by delegation, rather than by the cumbersome method of amending the *Papua and New Guinea Act* every time an extension of ministerial powers was required. The Administrator held powers and functions delegated to him by the Governor-General and could further delegate these to the Ministers of Papua New Guinea. Of course the delegation of powers made it possible also to withdraw them without exposing the process to criticism in the Australian Parliament, but, although some critics were unkind enough to attribute such base motives to the Government, the intention was merely to provide a simple and rapid means of extending the powers of the Ministers of Papua New Guinea as devolution proceeded. On no occasion was a power withdrawn after it had been delegated. No matter how reluctantly the Papua New Guinean Ministers accepted Gorton's challenge to manage their own affairs, an entirely new relationship between Australia and Papuan New Guinea was clearly in the making.

In other ways, in the first half of 1970, Papua New Guinea did not seem to present too many attractions to future Administrators. There was a virtual insurrection in the Gazelle Peninsula on the island of New Britain, where the Tolai people were riven by internal strife. A large dissident group had formed the Mataungan Association[9] in opposition to the legally constituted Gazelle local government council and to the colonial administration. There had been violent confrontations and over one thousand riot police had been despatched there to attempt to control the situation. There were fears that even this show of strength would be insufficient and that the use of troops might be necessary.

The island of Bougainville was another trouble spot.

The development of a large copper mine by the Australian-based company Conzinc Riotinto of Australia Ltd (CRA) had aroused separatist feelings, never far below the surface among Bougainvilleans. What had looked like a possible bonanza for Papua New Guinea in terms of development and financial benefit now seemed more likely to lead to a strong secessionist movement in Bougainville.

Morale in the Papua New Guinea Public Service was low; the younger, better educated Papua New Guineans were restless at the slow pace of localization. Section 49 of the Public Service Ordinance designed to provide for promotion preference for indigenous officers had not once been implemented. Expatriate officers were equally uneasy at the threat to their position, and the apparent inability of the Australian Government to come up with a satisfactory compensation scheme for loss of career if their positions were localized. An acceptable compensation scheme would have to precede much acceleration in the rate of localization. The need for such a scheme had been apparent for almost ten years but it stayed in the "too hard", basket because the Australian Treasury managed to reject all of the proposals put forward.

The Whitlam visit had caused repercussions and dissension throughout the politically conscious segment of the population. This was reflected in the House of Assembly. Traimya Kambipi, the member for Kompiam-Baiyer in the Western Highlands District, remarked with some cynicism, "I am sure that Mr Whitlam's visit was for the good of his own party",[10] and Yauwe Wauwe, another highlander from the Chimbu District, said "They [my people] said that what Mr Whitlam suggested about independence in 1972 was too early . . . they told me . . . that independence was in the hands of their members."[11] Concerned about the divisive effect of the issues raised by Whitlam, Matiabe Yuwi, another highlander from the Southern Highlands District, said "I do not like to see division among ourselves. We must have a unified country with one united people living in it . . . if there is dissension among ourselves we will not get anywhere."[12]

The gospel according to Whitlam had certainly created a sharp division between the young Papua New Guinean public servants, many of them undertaking courses at the Administrative College, and the conservative majority in the House of Assembly. It was perhaps coincidental that at this time the Papua New Guinea Public Service Board, exercising its independence of the Administrator and his Council, chose to rename this critically important institution which had been the "Administrative College" since its foundation, and dub it prosaically the "Public Service Training Centre". For once, members of the House of Assembly were united and promptly moved to introduce a Bill to restore the original name, which the Chairman of the Public Service Board, Gerald Unkles, labelled as political interference in the Board's prerogative. The Bill was passed and the original name was restored, though we had to work hard to dissuade the Department of Territories from counselling the Minister to have it disallowed. Percy Chatterton's words, in supporting the Bill, are indicative of the strong feelings aroused: "Let us make the change before the place collapses altogether and let us hope that, after this restoration of name has been effected, it will be possible to build up the internal morale and the external prestige to the position they once held."[13]

In other respects, too, and quite apart from the measures announced by the Prime Minister in mid—1970, politics in Papua New Guinea, as evidenced within the House of Assembly and the tertiary education institutions, seemed close to a take-off point of their own volition. The second House of Assembly had been elected in 1968 and, although its membership did not materially change the conservative nature of the House, there were a number of younger and better educated members, a number of individuals with a positive attitude towards managing their own affairs. There were also the beginnings of political parties. The Pangu Pati (Papua and New Guinea Union) had its origins during the first House of Assembly and was officially launched in June 1967. In the second House, though Pangu Pati numbers were still few, perhaps a fluctuating dozen, it could usually muster a number of fellow travellers to provide an opposition that could not be ignored. After the 1968 election we had in mind the appointment of some Ministerial Members from the Pangu Pati but the party rejected these proposals, preferring to be independent of government decisions. Pangu was well led in the House by Michael Somare, with strong support from Tony Voutas, Ebia Olewale, Pita Lus and others. In November 1969 Voutas had some sensible things to say to the majority who opposed Pangu policies on political development.

> I think that the conservative case can no longer rest on an anti-party fear . . . the only action open to the conservatives . . . is for them also to form a political party. It is my belief that by becoming a political party and presenting the people of Papua New Guinea with a conservative platform, you have honest politics. And further I would say that the only real way the ministerial member system can work is if it is based on a majority party or a coalition majority party.[14]

In 1970 the conservatives, to whom Voutas referred, took his advice and formed a political party originally called Compass, but later to become the United Party, claiming a membership of forty-seven in a House of eighty-four elected members and ten official members. Shortly afterwards a middle-of-the-road party appeared, the People's Progress Party, led by Julius Chan, and claiming eleven members in the House.

The development of Pangu in particular made essential a change in relationship between the Minister for External Territories and his Canberra bureaucrats, and the Papua New Guinea administration. There was now a well organized, articulate opposition voice to Australian Government policies in Papua New Guinea. It was small but strongly based among the younger and better educated segment of the population, men and women from whom would be drawn the future leaders of the country. The party was also strongly supported among the academics at the University and the Institute of Higher Technical Education. The Australian Minister and his advisers were slow to see this opposition, and the importuning of David Hay for devolution of decision-making to local hands had gone largely unheard until the flurry of activity following the Whitlam visit, culminating in the Gorton initiatives in July 1970.

The House of Assembly had pre-occupations other than those of pure politics. It had settled down to be a responsible body which, to the official members, meant pretty general support for the policies advocated. The Ministerial Members individually did not show much evidence of original thought nor any strong propensity to take initiatives. The most active Ministerial Members were, probably, Matt Toliman in Education, Tore Lokoloko in Health and Oala Oala Rarua in Treasury, but prior to July 1970 the reins had been far too firmly held by the Canberra-based Minister and his officials to encourage the exercise of initiative. The opportunities extended to them by John Gorton seemed unlikely to produce significant changes in the power structure.

Other matters which particularly attracted the attention of the House during the first half of 1970 included,
first, the education reforms designed to draw together
into one teaching service teachers from both Administration and mission schools, with the entire system
overseen by an Education Board, representative of all of
the previously separate education organizations. At this
time there were some fifty separate mission organizations registered in Papua New Guinea. The requisite
Bills introduced by the Ministerial Member for Education, Toliman, an ex-mission teacher himself, were
warmly supported by Michael Somare, the leader of
Pangu, and an ex-administration teacher. The Bills
passed without opposition.[15]

Much debate in the House focussed on the problems
in the Gazelle Peninsula, with Oscar Tammur, member
for Kokopo and the patron of the Mataungan Association (MA), taking up large segments of the Hansard
record of debates. "The MA realizes that the people of
the Gazelle Peninsula are dissatisfied over a lot of
things. Both the MA and the pro-multiracial council
group have difficulties. There is nothing we can do at
present that will unite these two groups of people. I
cannot possibly find a way."[16] (Neither could the
Administration.)

With the visit of Whitlam still fresh in the minds of
members, the possible timing of self-government and
independence got frequent airings, as did criticism of
the statements of that eminent visitor, as offered, for
instance, by John Middleton, member for Sumkar in the
Madang District.

Last Christmas . . . Mr Whitlam came here. Mr
Whitlam said "I want to go to see Papua New Guinea. I
wish to go to hear the opinions of these people to see
what their worries are." But when the plane came to
Port Moresby he spoke to reporters, before he had seen

ꞌany of the local people — yet he said "when I become Prime Minister in 1972 I will give self-government to Papua New Guinea. In 1976 I will give independence to Papua New Guinea."

He did not come and ask us even though he said he wanted to see the native people. Before he came he made these declarations. He did not mention the Constitutional Committee which has been established to seek the views of the people. He did not listen to the Constitutional Committee; he is not worried about it.[17]

The need for the restoration of capital punishment was an ever-present preoccupation of the members from the less developed districts. One clause of a motion from Momei Pangial, member for Mendi in the Southern Highlands, read: "That this House requests the Administration to introduce legislation making death, or at least life imprisonment, a mandatory punishment for persons convicted of wilful murder."[18] A fellow Southern Highlands member from the remote Huri Valley, Andrew Wabiria, went further: "My constituents support this suggestion of hanging murderers in public."[19]

On a sartorial note was Pita Lus' preoccupation with appropriate parliamentary dress — "I see that some members are wearing coloured shirts on the floor of the Chamber. Can something be done to ensure that our parliament is respected by wearing white shirts?"[20]

Finally, on the last day of the June 1970 meeting of the House, Paul Lapun, member for South Bougainville, produced a surprise by presenting a Sorcery Bill. "We ourselves, the people of this country, know that sorcery does occur."[21]

These problems and preoccupations were hardly new to me, for I had been an official member of the House of Assembly sinces its inception in 1964, and its leader for the past two years. I had been a member of both the Select Committees on Constitutional Development established by the House and was, as well, a member of the Administrator's Executive Council.

These various responsibilities had made me pretty well known in Papua New Guinea, while many of the influential men in the House were my personal friends and frequent guests at my house. Also, with the localization of senior public service positions now a key policy development, my term as Director of Education between 1962 and 1966 became an important advantage. In 1963 the Department of Education had set up a programme to develop indigenous education executives and out of this came many of the first men sufficiently qualified and experienced to be considered for senior postings throughout the Administration. Two of them became the first Papua New Guineans to be appointed as Departmental Heads — Paulias Matane and Sere Pitoi.[22] Other members of our initial course were also to assume prominence in the wider spheres of government. Michael Somare became the first Prime Minister, Alkan Tololo the first indigenous Director of Education, and later Chairman of the Public Service Board, and Aisea Taviai became Director of the Department of Lands. Vincent Eri, the first Papua New Guinean novelist and later a High Commissioner to Australia, was also a teacher. He is presently Head of the Department of Defence. Oala Oala Rarua, another ex-teacher, was Papua New Guinea's first High Commissioner to Australia.

I had also acted as Administrator during David Hay's absence on leave and overall felt reasonably well prepared for whatever might befall, and drew some spurious encouragement from various newspaper reports welcoming my appointment. I was delighted, but not a little surprised, to note that an editorial had attributed to me previously unsuspected qualities of "integrity, sagacity and a deep humanity".[23]

In the period between the announcement of my appointment and the date for taking up duty the Australian Government despatched me to New York as an adviser to the Australian delegation to the UN Trusteeship Council hearing on the Trust Territory of New Guinea. My fellow advisers were two Papua New Guineans, Jack KaruKuru from the Gulf District and Aloysius Noga from Bougainville. Apart from some mild harassment from the U.S.S.R. delegate, my modest duties were despatched without incident, and I travelled to Africa to see how some of Britain's ex-colonies were making out, specifically Ghana and Tanzania; Papua New Guinea's Select Constitutional Committee, of which I had previously been a member, was also roaming the world and I met up with them in Tanzania. They

Swearing-in of the Administrator of Papua New Guinea, at Government House, Canberra, 21 July 1970. From left: Tore Lokoloko, Aide to the Governor-General, Sinake Giregire, O.I. Ashton, Dulcie Johnson, Sir Paul Hasluck, Les Johnson, Secretary to Governor-General, Lady Hasluck, C.E. Barnes, George Warwick Smith.

had just come from Uganda, where at least some of the group found some elements of the after-hours hospitality a little embarrassing!

It was not until I reached Singapore on the way home that I saw an Australian newspaper which brought me down to earth because headlines described serious trouble in the Gazelle Peninsula, and the despatch of further large police reinforcements. My wife and I spent a couple of days in Canberra to be sworn in by the Governor-General, Paul Hasluck (previously long time Minister for Territories), to catch up with events with officers of the Department of External Territories and to consider priorities.

Obviously I would have to give immediate attention to defusing the Gazelle situation. However as my principal, but undefined, function would be to ensure a smooth and speedy movement to self-government, there would need to be rapid progress in the localization of the public service; Ministerial Members would have to be encouraged to exercise the powers recently devolved upon them; and the Constitutional Committee would need some impetus to come up with reasonably early target dates for independence.

I was optimistic enough to believe that these were attainable objectives.

NOTES

1. The term "Ministerial Member" for elected members of the Papua New Guinea House of Assembly holding quasi-Ministerial office was insisted on in 1967 by the Australian Government which felt that the term "Minister" was inappropriate to the responsibilities exercised. Locally we always referred to them as Ministers.
2. Notes of the 1970 Constitutional Committee meeting transmitted to Papua New Guinea by letter, undated, PP.
3. LH4717 1 February 1970, PP.

4. See Chapter 3.
5. ' Draft, 7 May 1970, PP.
6. Teleprint message, 22 January 1970, PP.
7. *Steps Towards Self-Government in Papua New Guinea*, speech by the Prime Minister at Papua Hotel, Port Moresby, 6 July 1970, AGPS, Canberra, 20176/70.
8. The much-amended Act, finally the *Papua New Guinea Act* 1949–75, was repealed by the *Papua New Guinea Independence Act* 1975.
9. "Mataungan" is a Kua nua word variously translated as "Watch out" or "be alert".
10. P.N.G., House of Assembly Debates (HAD), vol. II, no. 9, p. 2280.
11. Ibid., p. 2283.
12. Ibid., p. 2317.
13. P.N.G., HAD, vol. II, no. 10, p. 2938.
14. P.N.G., HAD, vol. II, no. 7, p. 1906.
15. P.N.G., HAD, vol. II, no. 10, pp. 2681, 2808.
16. P.N.G., HAD, vol. II, no. 9, p. 2433.
17. Ibid., p. 2605.
18. P.N.G., HAD, vol. II, no. 10, p. 2966.
19. Ibid., p. 2970.
20. P.N.G., HAD, vol. II, no. 9, p. 2570.
21. P.N.G., HAD, vol. II, no. 10, p. 2959.
22. Matane then served as Papua New Guinea Ambassador to the U.S.A. and the UN and currently is Secretary of the Department of Foreign Affairs; Pitoi became the first indigenous Chairman of the Public Service Board.
23. *Post Courier*, Port Moresby, 6 May 1970.

3

FIRST THINGS

My wife and I arrived in Port Moresby on 23 July 1970 to a warm but wet welcome, the rain effectively eliminating a good deal of the pomp and ceremony that had been arranged. The next day I was at work.

I came to the post of Administrator relatively un-encumbered with obligations and remarkably free of driving instructions. The *Papua and New Guinea Act* required that the Administrator be appointed by the Governor-General and be subject to his direction, which meant, of course, being directed by, and respon-sible to, the Minister for External Territories. The per-sonality of that Minister, his industry, his interest and background knowledge, obviously influenced the way in which the Administrator carried out his duties. Paul Hasluck, the Minister for Territories from 1951 to the end of 1963, exercised the firmest control on his public service officers in both Canberra and Papua New Guinea, but his successor, C.E. Barnes, was less well-equipped to do so and much more prepared to accept the policies and advice pressed upon him by the per-manent secretary of his Department, George Warwick Smith. The disappearance of Smith and the accession of David Hay to the post changed the Canberra/Moresby relationship much more towards an equal partnership.

Perhaps as a last hurrah, Smith rather than the Minister, signed a direction to me when I took up the post; it was but a shadow of his past endeavours. It contained only two firm guidelines. I was in complete agreement with both of them and needed no injunctions to motivate me to do my best to implement them. They were:

> The Government considers that the existing policy of increasing the extent to which the native people participate in political social and economic affairs needs to be given a great deal more bite.
>
> *and*
>
> The Government has also directed that those Commonwealth Departments and Agencies now performing functions of internal self-government outside the aegis of the Administrator should be reviewed so that a sensible programme of absorption in appropriate cases into the Territory Administration may be prepared.[1]

The Mataungan Association was certainly participating vigorously in the political, social and economic affairs of the Gazelle Peninsula. It was my first preoccupation. There were some 60,000 Tolais in the Gazelle Peninsula, and at that time there were over one thousand police in the area to discourage violence on the part of members of the Association and to prevent illegal entries of plantations by squatters, to protect the property of the local government council and of cocoa fermentaries and the like. The Administration had, in reserve, authority to call upon the defence forces for assistance should it be necessary, for the Mataungans could muster some thousands of followers for demonstrations, though they had never shown any real disposition to take on the police.

The initiative for the creation of the Mataungan Association came from Oscar Tammur, though its roots lie deep in the Tolai past, in the economic pressures on a rapidly increasing population and the disintegration of traditional Tolai society. In 1967 Tammur was a young man of twenty-six years of age. He had been a teacher, then a member of the Pacific Islands Regiment. On his discharge he returned home and set his sights on winning a seat in the House of Assembly in the 1968 elections. To assist his campaign he harnessed the dissatisfactions of land hungry people and organized a group of villagers to move on to some unused land on an expatriate-owned plantation, where they began to plant up coconuts. They were evicted peaceably enough by the police but it was the beginning of a well organized opposition to the status quo. The discontent was channelled into a newly created group called the Mataungan Association, commonly known as the MA. Tammur became its patron. He also won a seat in the election.

There was a long history of dissatisfaction on the Gazelle Peninsula, beginning with the alienation of land during the German regime, the development of expatriate-owned plantations, and of Tolai cash cropping. The resultant pressures on land were vastly increased by the population explosion after World War II. The Mataungan movement was born of the strains imposed upon a relatively static social system by rapid economic development and by the availability of formal education for almost all Tolai children. Similar strains were apparent in other parts of Papua New Guinea, but the particular features of the Gazelle Peninsula produced a movement unique in its strength, cohesion and durability. The concentration of population and the good road system, allied to the widespread ownership of motor vehicles, contributed to the welding together of an effective mass movement and to its control by leaders. An additional source of strength was the growing number of landless, unemployed youth, ready adherents to any anti-establishment movement with elements pandering to emotion and hysteria.

The fertility of the soil in the Gazelle and the availability of facilities for the preparation and sale of copra and cocoa had made the Tolai the most affluent of all Papua New Guineans, but it had also increased the land hunger, and sharpened their perception of the economic gulf between the expatriate planter and the Tolai farmer. The high birth-rate among the Tolai and increasing educational opportunities intensified long-standing resentment at foreign intrusion. Intrusion, and resistance to it, are well documented in Tolai mythology.

Factors underlying the Mataungan movement were complex, but land was the focal point of dissatisfaction. Land alienation to foreigners, whether by freehold title as in German times, or by leasehold, more recently, was one point where all Tolais came together with a common point of view and a common sense of injustice. But the movement was full of contradictions, and the statements of its leaders were often sharply at odds, and were frequently quite irrational. Traditional village feeling included a desire to turn back to the old days and the old ways, and here sorcery as well as violence was legitimate in enforcing compliance. It was present in the MA. On the other hand the majority of leaders also wanted to take over the complex economic machine which produced wealth for expatriates, though this would mean the flouting of traditional ways. Land ownership statements were evidence of this contradiction. Some MA leaders at times advocated the abolition of the traditional matriachal land inheritance system, and at others its retention.

Tammur's organization of the squatters was a spark which ignited many grievances, and one which burned very brightly was the enlargement of the boundaries of

the local government council which led to the inclusion
of four expatriates on what had previously been an all-
Tolai Council.[2] There were forty-two councillors in all,
so that the expatriate dilution was not significant to
foreign eyes, but the all-Tolai council had existed since
1963 and had evolved from five separate councils
which had been set up in 1951. The old council itself
had approved its dissolution in favour of a multiracial
council, but, as it was Administration policy at this time
for local government councils to go multiracial, no
doubt the Tolai council had been subject to some per-
suasion from Administration officers to make the
change. There were plenty of voices urging caution and
suggesting that the Tolai reaction could be quite hostile
but they went unheeded. The multiracial council
(MRC) became a bone in the MA's throat and the
initials "MRC" were transmuted to "Masta rules
council". The then Administrator, David Hay, and I,
with a number of Papua New Guinean Ministerial
Members, visited Rabaul in 1969 for a normal meeting
of the Executive Council and to meet the new
multiracial council, whereupon the MA gave us a taste
of things to come by mounting a mass demonstration
outside the Council Chambers, chanting slogans under
the baton of Oscar Tammur. When the ceremony in the
building concluded, largely unheard because of noises
off, we were met by a mass of hostile bodies. The
crowd made a grudgingly narrow pathway for us to
pass to our waiting vehicles. It was only ten metres but
it seemed a long journey. Thereafter the MA was in
total opposition to the MRC and all its works, including
the highly profitable co-operative, the Tolai Cocoa
Project, which had serviced Tolai cocoa farmers
throughout the Gazelle, including, of course many
adherents of the MA.

I considered the problem on the morning of 24 July

1970. At that stage the situation was as follows: There had been squatters on undeveloped land to which title was held by some plantation owners and there was a threat of more squatters to come. There had been widespread refusal to pay taxes to the MRC and little prospect of a change of heart. Violence had been inflicted upon council supporters and counter violence on members of the MA. The Tolai themselves were irrevocably split into those who supported the council (the establishment) and those who opposed it, the rebel MA. Organized harassment of council activities had taken place and there had been Administrative action against MA incursions on, and damage to, privately-owned and council property. The Administration had prosecuted tax defaulters and, as they refused to pay either fines or taxes, some, including Oscar Tammur, went to prison.

In short, the Administration's response had been to use available legal sanctions to protect property and to support the legally-established council. We needed a thousand armed police to do it.

We had attempted some more constructive responses, notably the release of some Administration land for distribution to the landless, and the purchase of some freehold properties, the plantations of Matanatar and Revalien, for a similar purpose. There were plans to establish a land board to allocate the blocks, but so far no one had received a plot of land. There didn't seem to be many favourable options. On the one hand we could mobilize more force, and I had authority to call upon the Papua New Guinea Defence Force if required. The Defence Forces, though largely indigenous, were part of the Australian Defence Force, subject to control by the three Australian Service Ministers under the overall jurisdiction of the Minister for Defence. Each of them was particularly sensitive to the political dangers of the use of troops to quell civil disturbances and it was an unusual concession that had been extended to us, though usage was still surrounded by precautionary restrictions. The only other option appeared to be to try to develop the rather meagre constructive initiatives we had taken.

As an immediate precaution I had prepared a letter to the respective Commanders of the Navy, Army and Air Force detachments stationed in Papua New Guinea. My letter was undated and read:

> From reports received by me today from Rabaul I am satisfied that a confrontation or serious incident has occurred which in my judgment threatens or shows loss of control of the situation by the police. I therefore requisition such military forces as you consider to be necessary for the maintenance of public peace in the Gazelle Peninsula and in the Territory of Papua and New Guinea.[3]

The letter was put away in my safe for use should the situation deteriorate. Fortunately there was no occasion for its despatch.

Despite this precautionary measure, I did not think that any possible future disturbance would need a thousand police to contain it, and I hoped that a positive gesture such as the withdrawl of a significant number of riot squads might reduce the temperature. This step, followed up by a personal visit, might make a dialogue possible. The previous total intransigence of the MA did not seem to offer much ground for optimism, but a fresh start by a new Administrator who was well known in the Gazelle might produce some headway. Not long before I left Papua New Guinea, earlier in the year, I had visited Rabaul and had attended and addressed a meeting of all of the MA leaders of the individual villages, without, it must be said, making any impression on them, but at least I knew many of the leaders personally. There seemed to be at least a chance of progress. I discussed the matter over the telephone with David Hay, now established in the Department of External Territories, and we agreed to give it a try. I planned a three-day visit to Rabaul.

First, we announced a reduction in police strength and the dates for my visit (5, 6 and 7 August) and my wish to speak with the MA leaders. These men varied in their responses. John Kaputin undertook to arrange a meeting but Damien Kereku said that no meeting would take place. ABC radio quoted him as saying that I was "just another Administration official implementing the Australian Prime Minister's policies," and that "we have met Mr Johnson and achieved nothing, another meeting is pointless."[4] However, I hoped for at least some informal talks. I had a crowded three days.

First, I met the legally-constituted multiracial council, which was very firm in its intention to maintain its position and called upon the Administration to enforce the law, to increase prosecutions for failure to pay council tax and to maintain order, for which they wanted greater police strength. Nothing very constructive came out of the meeting; members felt as they were the legally constituted council it was up to the Administration to protect their position.

After much dithering the MA decided that they would meet me, which was at least one step forward, and nine members of their executive came along, though Oscar Tammur evaded the issue by disappearing to the Duke of York islands. We had a friendly discussion in which they said that they were willing to have discussion with anybody in the Gazelle Peninsula to solve the current problem, their only condition being the revocation of the multiracial council proclamation. I was sceptical and recorded in my account of the visit:

> There was, and is, no indication that their fundamental attitudes have changed. In short, I suspect that when

discussions did begin, they would simply insist that they were quite capable of governing the affairs of the Gazelle Peninsula themselves on their own ideas and their principles, and discussions would break down.[5]

The basic issue was which faction would control the Gazelle and no compromise seemed possible at that time.

I had also arranged to show the Administration flag in the Mataungan strongholds by visiting them as in the normal course of a visit. Administration officers were concerned that this might lead to hostile demonstrations but conditions seemed quite normal. I had a friendly visit to schools in Matupit and Kapakap villages with parents on hand (MA followers to a man), to escort me around and to be photographed together under the school flag.

I also met representatives of the expatriate community who were anxious to avoid involvement in what they regarded as an Australian/Tolai problem. Next I saw members of the Warmaran Association, whose members were senior Tolai public servants striving to mediate but inevitably linked with the Administration as far as the MA was concerned. One of their recommendations which we took up later was that a greater number of Tolai public servants should be posted to the Gazelle. Next was the Warbete Association who had long stood out of all council affairs and continued to stand apart from the warring factions. All the Warbete members wanted was to be left entirely alone to manage their own affairs with their own money, but with the cautionary provision that the Administration would, of course, continue to provide schools, teachers, medical care and so on. Then I had discussions with a group of "big men", mostly elderly Tolais whose influence was being eroded by the younger radicals. It was clear to me that their day had passed.

About the only really positive result was a meeting with the village committee on the allocation of blocks of land from the two plantations we had purchased, Matanatar and Revalien. We sat around on a log in the bush and thrashed it out. I quote from my report of the meeting:

> There was general agreement among the community that Revalien should be divided into five-acre blocks and we agreed upon this with each village representative indicating acceptance of the plan. When questioned on attitudes concerning the disposal of Matanatar it appeared that each village had at least some people who supported the big block plantation solution, proposed originally by Oscar Tammur. [This was that the plantation would remain as one unit but under a management representing the villagers.] We reached the conclusion that the best thing to do was to delay for a short period of time a final decision on Matanatar to see if the plantation group could come up with enough capital to operate the whole area, or part of it, as a going concern. Everybody seemed to be quite happy with this solution — indeed rather relieved that the whole thing had been settled more or less finally at last.[6]

I got a lot of satisfaction out of this grass-roots democracy, as well as some helpful newspaper publicity. However, my conclusions after three days of intensive discussions were not optimistic. I summarized them in the report previously quoted.

> In my view the only possibility of a solution within the relatively near future would be the revocation of the proclamation establishing the multiracial Council. In view of the strong Council attitude, however, I would not like to exert undue pressure on the Council to reach the same conclusion but rely upon the pressure of public opinion in the Gazelle Peninsula which seems to be tending in this direction. However one should not be too optimistic about what might happen once the

proclamation is revoked. There would certainly be strong pressure on the Mataungans to assist in coming to some sort of satisfactory solution, but their intransigence in the past does not suggest that they would be likely to budge, if indeed a conference did eventuate . . . I am not optimistic of much immediate significant improvement.[7]

The Administration was responsible for peace and order in Papua New Guinea. It could not grant the demands of a movement representing perhaps half of the population of the Gazelle when these demands were hotly contested by the other half. I could see only three options; concede to the MA demands, which would place it in effective control of the Gazelle; suppress the MA, to which similar objections applied (this, at any rate, did not seem possible except by the use of very considerable force and perhaps with serious injuries and loss of life); or to continue what might be termed an armed truce, while keeping open lines of communication among the parties: the Papua New Guinea Government, the multiracial council supporters and the MA. Such a truce would be punctuated by occasional incidents such as squatter activity and disruption of work at cocoa fermentaries and the like and would require continued large police presence, but we opted for it.

The MA's riposte came in December 1970 when Damien Kereku, as Chairman of the Association, conveyed to me formally a resolution of the Association:

That the Administration be informed that the native people of the Gazelle Peninsula no longer have the slightest confidence in the Administration of Papua New Guinea and that they are severing themselves from the Administration's policies in matters relating to the social, political, economic and land development in the Gazelle Peninsula and that the natives will have to shoulder as best they can any responsibiltiy for development in these fields.[8]

Fine sentiments, though it must be borne in mind that the MA did not speak for a majority of the Tolai people.

Meanwhile prominence began to be given to the newly-established economic arm of the MA named the New Guinea Development Corporation (NGDC). Shares were sold to supporters and the intention was to set up a variety of business activities, the first of which was to be competitive with the Tolai Cocoa Project which was associated with the legally constituted council and its supporters. Despite the damage to the long established Cocoa Project likely to be caused by the NGDC there was a cautious welcome for the more positive direction in which the MA appeared to be moving. The Association's ambitious plan was ultimately to buy back the economy from the whites, first by vigorous economic competition, and by economic boycott, and ultimately, if necessary, by expropriation. But it was a long time getting established and disturbances continued.

As I had undertaken in my discussions with the Gazelle Peninsula villagers concerning the disposal of the two plantations we had purchased, Matanatar and Revalien, they were divided into two-hectare blocks and allocated to individuals. Concurrently we agonized over the only other obvious initiative to be taken — the withdrawal of the Proclamation establishing the multi-racial council. But in January 1971 the Administrator's Executive Council bit on the bullet and directed that the Gazelle council revert to all-Tolai membership. Nonetheless disorder continued. There were attempts to occupy cocoa fermentaries owned by the Tolai Cocoa Project and obstruction of activities on Administration and privately-owned land, so that ultimately I decided to enlist outside advice. I chose Professor R.F. Salisbury, then at McGill University, an anthropologist who was well known for his previous work among the Tolai and who would be seen to be entirely free of the taint of any association with the Administration or the Australian Government. Salisbury was a bit surprised to be asked to undertake the role of adviser but pleased to have an opportunity to get back among the Tolai. He spent August of 1971 on the job and reported promptly. I did not expect him to offer a solution to the Gazelle imbroglio on a platter and indeed the generality of his recommendations did not offer anything new nor much that had not been previously considered and in many cases implemented. We felt that we had tried everything to resolve the situation except capitulation to MA demands. On any number of occasions a referendum had been suggested to determine what sort of local government the majority desired, but we insisted that it be conducted by secret ballot, which the MA rejected. Acquired land had been distributed, and we were proceeding with more acquisitions. I had offered to appoint a member of the MA to the Land Board which was allocating blocks on the acquired land. I had directed Administration Departments to appoint Tolais, to executive positions in Rabaul, where possible, though I had some reservations about this as it would tend to enclave the Tolai, whereas our efforts were being directed towards the creation of a national consciousness. A good many Tolais proved reluctant to return to their homeland where, inevitably, they would get embroiled in the bitter faction quarrel. But the real substance of Salisbury's report was that the Administration should generate a new approach to the MA and not continue to separate Tolais into "goodies" and "baddies".

This suggestion may have borne some fruit, but on 19 August a group of villagers planned and executed the murder of Jack Emanuel, the District Commissioner. Emanuel was accompanying a police party investigating a report of illegal occupation of privately-owned land. He was lured away from the police on the pretext that he was needed to explain Administration actions to a group of villagers. There he was stabbed in the back with an old bayonet and died while attempting to regain the protection of the police party.

The shock wave spread through the whole country. There were theories that Emanuel's murder was related to an affray in the Gazelle Peninsula in August 1958 when he was present when two Tolais were shot dead. Some saw it as an open challenge to the Australian Administration which could lead to the takeover of the Gazelle by the Tolai people and the eviction of all the whites. Others considered it an isolated, irrational episode inspired by sorcery and conspiracy. The Tolais themselves were deeply shocked and Emanuel was given an emotional funeral in which thousands of Tolais from all contending groups took part.

From the whites there were cries for reprisals, among the Tolais fear that the police would be let loose in the villages. I set out to quell one group and to reassure the others in two broadcasts, one immediately after the news of the murder was received, and a second in Rabaul after the funeral. I spoke in English and Pidgin with an interpreter also rendering it in Kua nua, the Tolai language.

From Port Moresby I said:

Today a brave and a good man has died. Jack Emanuel has served Papua New Guinea faithfully and well for twenty-five years. Now he is dead. He is dead because he believed and he trusted.

I know that all the people of Papua New Guinea will view this terrible act with horror and revulsion. Whether its causes lie in the remote or in the recent past does not matter now. But is not this the time for all people to abjure violence? Is it not a time to settle our differences, large and small, by negotiation, by dis-

cussion and by compromise? Have we not learned the
bitter lesson that violence solves nothing, concludes
nothing? It feeds on itself until it becomes a monster
that devours us all. May I urge that the leaders in the
Gazelle Peninsula will confirm that they follow the
paths of peace.

We all grieve at the consequences of this mindless
act. A woman and her children have lost a loving
husband and father. Papua New Guinea has lost a
faithful servant. We have all lost a man, a man indeed.[9]

In Rabaul I spoke at much greater length. Two
paragraphs follow:

But this deed is done and cannot be undone. Its effects
cannot be undone. People are afraid. They are afraid
because they do not know what lurks in the dark
recesses of their own minds or in the minds of their
neighbours. What do the people of the Gazelle need
most now? I think it is quite clear, above all they need
freedom from fear.

The Government will give them freedom from fear.
But any Government can only do this if the people
help. A Government is of the people and for the people
and it cannot operate without the help of the people.
Police alone cannot ensure freedom from fear. The
police, and the people, and the courts, and all of the
apparatus of government must work together if the
Gazelle is to be freed from fear. We look to you to help
us to banish fear from your hearts.

I added a concluding homily:

If you are to influence national government you must
speak with one voice. Now you speak with many. It is
not for me to tell you how to speak with one voice. It is
for you, but you cannot be strong like you are. What
are you going to do about it? You, yourselves, must
now decide whether to be divided and weak, or united
and strong![10]

Fortunately the man who struck the fatal blow was
arrested shortly afterwards, though it seems that he was

almost as much an instrument of others as the bayonet he wielded. He was sentenced to eleven years imprisonment, and some others, whose involvement was proven, also received prison sentences. In reviewing the situation in October, I wrote:

> If the villages fear is the dominant emotion, fear of violence from MA followers if the people do not conform to MA direction, and fear of harsh reprisals from the Administration. The only organized coherent group in the Peninsula with firm leadership is the Mataungan Association, and in the villages it can enforce compliance by the use of intimidation. Complaints of stand-over tactics are few because police presence in some hundreds of villages is not possible and reprisals would follow any such complaints. The only effective counter to such tactics is the growth of an opposition movement using similar methods based on strong emotional grounds. There seems little possibility of this and in consequence the Government position, that the quarrel is between two Tolai groups, is hardly tenable. In the minds of most people the MA is opposed to the Government.[11]

Despite the antagonisms and the violent incidents, there was also a curious ambivalence in the relationships between the Tolai factions. I recall a farewell function my wife and I were given by the Tolai in Port Moresby on our departure from Papua New Guinea in April 1970, during which Toliman and Tammur, on opposite sides of the Tolai fence, sang a comradely duet. In October, all groups came together in Rabaul for Warwagira, an annual festival, which combined music, dancing, feasting and, in general, a display of Tolai culture, old and new. It included, for instance, a string band competition with almost every village entering a band, all of which played pop songs interminably. In contrast, there were magnificently arrayed warriors performing traditional dances. To my surprise I was asked to open the festival which I did, with good will on all sides, and an attempt on my part to define Tolai problems in allegorical terms.

> Society never stands still. When people meet new ideas, they accept some of them, reject some and their ways change to incorporate the new ideas. In Papua New Guinea in a very short space of time the people have been flooded with new ideas, new religions, new forms of government, new laws, new organizations, new machines. In some ways it has been like sitting down to a huge feast and trying to eat everything. Some of the food is tasty and we eat and enjoy. Some we don't like but being polite we try and eat it too. Then when we have eaten it all our stomach pains — we are uncomfortable and unhappy. Our stomach rebels and sometimes vomits it all forth. But next time when we eat the new food we choose what we want, and if we add it to our traditional food, our meal is enriched.
>   Life in Papua New Guinea has been like this. In many places people are still suffering from indigestion from trying to eat too many new ideas too quickly. In some places they have tried to replace all of the old traditional life with the new and are living a life which is neither nourishing nor satisfying. In other places they are now vomiting forth all the new ideas, both good and bad, that they have consumed too hastily.
>   It is very difficult to adjust and control our taste and our appetite for new things. Some people turn away from anything new and some will have none of the old. But sensible people take the best of the new and blend it with the old so that life becomes a rich and satisfying meal.[12]

Regrettably my oratorical efforts bore little fruit for, with Warwagira over, hostilities resumed, and by the end of 1971 I had come to the reluctant conclusion that a solution acceptable to the Government was quite unlikely to be achieved, and that our only recourse was a continuation of a policy of containment until a national Papua New Guinea Government inherited this legacy of colonialism. In a despatch to the Minister in January 1971 I wrote: "The Mataungan Association has already shown how difficult it is to counter civil disobedience movements on a large scale without recourse to a massive application of force and detention . . . such methods . . . cannot be applicable while Australia remains in a mentor position."[13]

It might be noted that in the national elections in March 1972 three of the four House of Assembly seats for the Gazelle were won by MA leaders — Kereku, its Chairman, Tammur, its patron, and Kaputin, who led the MA economic initiatives and also might be termed its polemicist, though Tammur was no slouch in this field. The fourth seat was retained by Toliman who had been a leading figure in Administration affairs as a member of the Administrator's Executive Council since 1964 and Ministerial Member for Education.

In fact the installation of a national government led by Michael Somare in April 1972 did not do much to resolve the Gazelle situation. The new ministry did its best to bring the contending parties together, which resulted in an agreement to abolish the local government council, only recently installed as an all-Tolai affair, and set up a management committee comprising members of all Tolai groups. The Minister for Local Government, Boyamo Sali, outlined the terms to the House of Assembly, and then revealed a Mataungan tactic familiar to the Administration:

> On the 25th May the Chief Minister received a telegram signed by Messrs Toliman and Tammur outlining an agreement reached by representatives . . . also personally signed by Mr Tomot on behalf of Mr Kereku. Mr Kereku was at the meeting but was not available when the telegram was sent. Mr Tomot sent a telegram to the Chief Minister on the same day asking

that his signature and that of Mr Tammur be dis-
regarded.[14]

Back to square one! The new Government was to
have as little success as the old one in dealing with the
MA, though, later, the inclusion of John Kaputin in the
Ministry relieved the position somewhat. At the same
meeting Kaputin railed at length at the injustice suffered
by the Tolais, some of it warranted, some self-
justification and some mere bombast. some extracts
follow:

Mr Speaker:
To date, much has been said about our opposition to
any form of local government on the Gazelle Peninsula.
With this in mind, Mr Speaker, my purpose in making
this statement is not to cast doubt on any attempt by
this government, which is about to inherit the laws of
an outgoing colonial power, but simply to attempt to
clarify our position, present or past, for I do not believe
that honourable members of this parliament can begin
to appreciate our views, or condemn the Tolai people,
without any understanding of the forces that have com-
pelled us to hold our present views in relation to the
subject now under considerable discussion . . .
   Before I go on, Mr Speaker, I would like to say that
very, very few tribes in this country have taken punishment equal to what the Tolai people have taken.
   We have received all sorts of things from condemna-
tion from the colonial power to facing police in protection of our land, from criticism by the press to abuse by
the white population and the business sector in this
country, from trusting a former Prime Minister of
Australia who held a gun by his side during his visit to
the Gazelle to having some of our people fatally shot
by the police at Navuneram.[15] . . . And now, of course,
five Tolai men have been sentenced to jail for terms
ranging from eighteen months to fourteen years for an
act, which, in my position as a Tolai, and knowing what
my people have taken or suffered, I now find myself
almost defenceless to define.

In addition to all this, Mr Speaker, our Tolai resources in terms of human power and natural resources have been exploited for the purpose of our country.

Yet, in return for all this, and for something for which we have no control, it seems to me, Mr Speaker, that to be a Tolai is almost like to be a pig in a pigsty where life of an animal depends, not on what is fit for human consumption, but on waste and remains, unfit for man . . . The terrible colour line which relegates the Papuans and New Guineans to a position of irremediable inferiority, the galling political domination, the attitude of the Westerners to substandard living, for which the Australians may not have been responsible, but towards which they remain largely indifferent, all this has left in this country a deep and even in the long run only slowly-healing wound.[16]

Relative calm return to the Gazelle only with the establishment of provincial government in Papua New Guinea a policy which permitted the establishment of satrapies throughout the country, including the Gazelle.

In retrospect our mistake was to apply a particular policy to the whole of Papua New Guinea, without taking into account the special circumstances in different parts of the country; that is, the decision that multiracial councils would be good things — a conclusion reached, and a policy applied, before the Australian Government had decided to hasten the arrival of self-government. In Rabaul the multiracial council decision, even though ostensibly reached by the old all-Tolai council, affronted the pride of very many Tolais and became a focal point for many other grievances, past and present.

NOTES

1. Smith to Administrator, 21 July 1970, PP.
2. Three Australian planters and one businessman of Chinese origin.

3. PP.
4. ABC Radio, *AM*, 4 August 1970.
5. Administrator to Secretary, Department of External Territories (DET), 10 August 1970, PP.
6. Ibid.
7. Ibid.
8. Letter, Kereku to Administrator, December 1970, PP.
9. Broadcast on ABC Radio, Port Moresby, 19 August 1971, PP.
10. Broadcast on Rabaul Radio, 21 August 1971, PP.
11. Memo, 16 October 1971, PP.
12. Administrator's address on opening of Warwagira in Rabaul, 8 October 1971, PP.
13. Despatch Administrator to Minister, 9 January 1971, PP.
14. P.N.G., House of Assembly Debates (HAD), vol. III, no. 2, p. 136.
15. This related to an affray in 1958 during which two Tolai were shot and killed.
16. P.N.G., HAD, vol. III, 23 June 1972.

4

POLITICS

The Gazelle Peninsula, though a continual worry, was not among the paramount concerns of the Administration. In an optimistic Christmas message broadcast on Christmas Day 1970, I was positively soothing. "It is true that, as well as the growth of national feeling, there were movements that tended to divide, weaken and separate our developing nation. I believe that these are passing phases and will not disrupt our march to nationhood."[1]

The major task facing the Administration was the implementation of the changes announced by the Prime Minister during his visit to Papua New Guinea in July 1970. The constitutional arrangements then in being were enshrined in the *Papua and New Guinea Act 1949–1968*, which had been amended to meet the recommendations of the Select Committee on Constitutional Development of the second House of Assembly. Section 24 of the Act provided for seven Ministerial Members and not more than ten Assistant Ministerial Members. Section 20 set out the constitution of the Administrator's Executive Council: the Administrator, three official members of the House of Assembly, the seven Ministerial Members and an elected non-ministerial member of the House of Assembly elected by the Administrator. Although the Assistant Ministerial Members were not members of the AEC, they possessed the same powers and responsibilities regarding their portfolios as did the Ministerial Members. Prior to the Gorton changes those powers were somewhat circumscribed.

> Each Minister [sic] should be responsible, with the permanent Departmental Head, for departmental policy, and for the over-all activities of the Department. The Minister would represent the Department in the House by answering questions, introducing and carrying legislation concerning his Department through all stages of proceedings, and by giving the departmental view on resolutions and motions affecting the Department. In the event of a disagreement between the Minister and the Departmental Head the matter should be referred to the Administrator for decision.[2]

Control was still firmly in the hands of an Australian Administration until Gorton swept it aside and thrust extensive and final powers upon Ministerial Members and Assistant Ministerial Members individually, and collectively upon that embryonic Cabinet, the Administrator's Executive Council.

At this time the members of the AEC, apart from myself, were:

Angmai Bilas — Trade and Industry
Oriel (Roy) Ashton — Works and Mining
Sinake Giregire — Posts and Telegraphs
Matthias Toliman — Education
Tei Abal — Agriculture, Stock and Fisheries
Tore Lokoloko — Public Health
Toua Kapena — Labour
Thomas Leahy — Administrator's nominee

Official members were Tony Newman, Tom Ellis and Jim Ritchie. The eight Assistant Ministerial Members were Andagari Wabiria, Joseph Lue, Kaibelt Diria, Meck Singiliong, Oala Oala Rarua, Lepani Watson, Siwi Kurondo and Wesani Iwoksim. The Ministry was balanced to give adequate representation to the four recognized Papua New Guinea regions. There were four members from Papua, five from the Highlands Districts, three from the New Guinea islands, and three from the New Guinea mainland (excluding the highlands). Leahy, the Administrator's nominee, was also from the New Guinea mainland. AEC members Ashton, Giregire, Abal and Toliman had all been members of the House of Assembly since 1964, the last three having played a prominent part in its affairs. Of the Assistant Ministerial Members, Diria, Watson and Kurondo were also members of the first House of Assembly. Giregire, Abal, Kurondo, Wabiria, Diria and Singiliong spoke little or no English, and in addition Kurondo and Diria, though speaking Pidgin fluently, could not read or write it with any competence.

One of the more cosmetic changes announced by the Prime Minister was that the AEC should have one of its elected members as its spokesman in the House of Assembly, "to answer questions as to what the AEC has done and why it has done it". This was a task previously carried out by the senior official member. It had been in the mind of my predecessor David Hay, that this job would fall to Tom Leahy. Leahy was an Australian, farming near the town of Lae in the Markham Valley, and a member of a rather numerous expatriate clan, most of whom were long-time residents in New Guinea. I personally thought that the trend of events indicated the need for an indigenous spokesman, but it was up to the members to make the decision themselves. We all met in Council on 19 August 1970 and discussed the nature of the task to be performed and the qualities required to handle it successfully then I and the other official members withdrew and left it to the elected members. There were two runners, Tom Leahy and Tore Lokoloko.[3] As Leahy appeared to have five of the eight votes sewn up, Lokoloko withdrew before a ballot, and as a consolation prize became Deputy Spokesman to Leahy.

The decision had a fairly lukewarm reception because it was expected that the position of spokesman would give the occupant an inside track on the top job when Papua New Guinea achieved self-government. But ambitious insiders were not too unhappy about it, for it was generally understood that an expatriate would have little prospect of leading an independent government and that the appointment of Leahy merely saved the day for prospective indigenous contenders. The strongest critic of the appointment was John Guise, then Speaker of the House of Assembly who, seeing the way the wind was blowing, had set out to get himself a firmer place in the radical wing of Papua New Guinean politics. He refused to recognize the legality of the position of Spokesman, and said that he would refer only to the Senior Official Member and not to the Spokesman. However, in the conduct of the House business at the succeeding meetings, Leahy's position was accepted by most of the members, and the Speaker did ultimately acknowledge his presence as Spokesman.

It did not take long to establish the mechanics of the Gorton devolution of the powers and responsibilities to Papua New Guinea, but the Papua New Guinean Ministers were far less ready to exercise those powers. The first six months of this new period saw Ministers hesitant to cast off the colonial bonds and be their own men, a reluctance which some of their expatriate departmental advisers did nothing to discourage. In fact, the magnitude of the changes passed almost unnoticed by the public, both in Papua New Guinea and Australia;

so much so that I devoted one of my weekly press conferences to explaining the comprehensive nature of the
powers now in the hands of local Ministers. By the end
of 1970 Ministers had taken little advantage of their
new authority. In a letter to the Minister of External
Territories in January 1971, I wrote:

> The outstanding event of the year was the constitu-
> tional change brought about by your determination
> under section 24 of the *Papua and New Guinea Act* which
> produced a large measure of home rule to Papua New
> Guineans. One of the important expectations was that
> Papuans and New Guineans would feel more involved
> in government and cease regarding the Administration
> as an oligarchy controlled and manipulated from
> Australia. . . . However total acceptance of the proposi-
> tion that it is a Papua New Guinea government and not
> a colonial administration depends on Ministerial office
> holders demonstrating a far greater degree of control of
> their portfolios and on them taking initiatives in deter-
> mining policies. Regrettably, to date individual
> Ministers have not shown that they have a good grasp
> of the problems of their departments and have not had
> sufficient self-confidence in their judgments to take
> policy initiatives.[4]

Matt Toliman, the Ministerial Member for Education, whom I regarded as one of the better and more
experienced members told his Departmental Head, Ken
McKinnon: "I'm better than you at putting our message
across to the people, but you must tell me what the
message is."[5]

Collectively, as an Administrator's Executive Council
we moved a little closer to the grand design.

> In collective deliberations within the AEC the perfor-
> mance of Ministerial Members has been a good deal
> better. There has been a very considerable growth in
> understanding the complex problems of Government
> and a readiness to press points of view strongly. In
> many areas members of the AEC still look for official

guidance but I think that it may be fairly claimed that the AEC is fulfilling its intended function in most areas of Government.[6]

But majority opinion in Papua New Guinea was still afraid to embrace the idea of self-determination. The words "self-government" were still anathema in most parts of the highlands, and people everywhere were alarmed at talk of target dates.

I set out to do what I could to move the highlanders into a more positive frame of mind by taking a trip through the Highlands Districts talking of self-reliance, of the capacity of highlanders to manage their own affairs, and to challenge their manhood, sometimes implying that they were acting like frightened children — "Long ting ting bilong mi yupela no man, manki tasol".[7] In the course of this visit we almost came to grief over the Chimbu mountains when the single engine of our plane failed, but the pilot managed to scrape in to the Kundiawa airstrip.

I'm not sure that I moved public opinion much, but at least I made the words "self-government" respectable and brought the issue into the open. Gough Whitlam called me the "shining exception"[8] in this regard, thus doing a good deal less than justice to very many of our officers who were loyally working to educate a reluctant populace to a new way of thinking about self-government. It must be said that some expatriate residents of Papua New Guinea still used "self-government" as scare words, but many Australian politicians carried a false "Sanders-of-the-river" stereotype in their minds when thinking and speaking about field officers in the Papua New Guinea service.

Other events helped to nudge forward the views of Papua New Guineans on self-government. These were two visits in close succession, the first by the leader of the Australian Labor Party, Gough Whitlam, following up his climactic visit of a year earlier, and the second the regular triennial inspection by a United Nations visiting mission.

In view of the furor created by the earlier Whitlam visit I was enjoined by the Minister for External Territories to make the most careful preparations for the visit, which commenced on 3 January 1971. The considerable party comprised Mr and Mrs Whitlam and Miss Whitlam, a sister of the leader, MHRs Cameron, Morrison and Keating and the President and Secretary of the ALP, Messrs. Burns and Young. I sent out a set of careful directions to the District Commissioners (DCs) of those Districts the party planned to visit to ensure contact with all shades of indigenous opinion, and equally to enjoin all DCs not to intrude on the party's activities. On the previous visit one unfortunate DC had incurred the wrath of the leader of the party by venturing to correct a misstatement made by the leader at a meeting. Extracts from my directions follow:

> The DC will arrange an evening reception for the party with representative District residents invited. Please ensure adequate representation of Papuans and New Guineans. DCs should arrange for a senior indigenous public servant to act as District host to Mr Whitlam and to interpret where necessary.
>
> DCs are expected to offer every assistance but to remain in the background unless their presence is required. DCs are not expected to be present at meetings arranged for the visitors.[9]

Whitlam was a good deal more restrained than in his previous visit. Prime Minister Gorton had stolen a deal of his thunder, while he had publicly approved the changes in the top structure of External Territories and the Papua New Guinea Administration. The party visited Port Moresby, Mount Hagen, Lae, Madang, Rabaul, Kieta and Alotau. There was nothing to rival the public rows of the earlier visit.

On this occasion the sharpest edge of the Whitlam tongue was directed towards the leaders of the highlands-based political party, Compass, which had been sponsored and supported by white settlers. Tei Abal, one of those leaders, responded by calling the distinguished visitor "a seven-day expert" who changed his tune to suit his audience and who was in the Territory to suit his own political ends.[10] Clyde Cameron upheld his reputation by airing some well-established prejudices, but on the whole I thought the visit had gone well. Papua New Guinea had been exposed to the views of an alternative Australian Government, and the visitors had sampled a wide cross-section of Papua New Guinean opinion. Whitlam's departing statement was certainly critical enough — it was, after all, a political document presenting the official position of Australia's parliamentary opposition party. Some extracts follow:

> In the past year the political climate of Papua New Guinea has been transformed. A year ago proposals for early self-government were met with official hostility and public dismay. Some elementary truths about the early and inevitable end of colonialism for Papua New Guinea held the terror of the unknown. Now the most significant leaders of Papua New Guinea and significant sections of the population accept that they must shortly come to terms with their own future as a self-governing nation. It has been a remarkable proof of the power of an idea. There can be no turning back now. . . . The Labor Party as a whole finds its most deeply held conscientious convictions affronted in Papua New Guinea. It would be impossible for a party like ours to condone or connive at vast inequalities, entrenched privilege, blatant exploitation and racial discrimination. These inescapable attributes of colonialism disfigure life in this colony. . . .
>
> In Papua New Guinea, it will be found increasingly that the question for the timing of self-government involves a quibble about a matter of two or three years.

Even if the Gorton Government were to survive, self-government will come in the lifetime of the next House of Representatives. The Australian Government has a clear duty to speed up preparations for the inevitable day. Target dates for self-government and independence should be set now, as we are obliged to do by the unopposed decision of the United Nations General Assembly. . . .

It may be true that men cannot be forced to be free; it is certainly true that men cannot be forced to rule others. An Australian Labor Government will not be blackmailed into accepting an unnatural role as rulers over those who have had no say and can have no say in electing us. Australia's obligation in the United Nations is to hand over Papua New Guinea as a single entity as soon as possible.[12]

A day or so after the visit I wrote to David Hay with my informal reactions to the visit. The first paragraph read:

The prepared statement issued on departure is not too much at variance with Government policy except on the insistence of a unilateral Australian decision and a rigid timetable. If the promises made by Mr Whitlam are implemented it would mean the establishment of self-government in Papua New Guinea at about the beginning of 1974 at the earliest. In the timetable we have in mind at the present, if there is a further devolution of power, then there will be a very substantial degree of self-government by 1974 in any case. It would seem to me that the Government could now emphasize that Papua New Guinea is already partly self-governing and in the light of the Select Committee's report, will move continuously towards total self-government as agreed between Papua New Guinea's representatives and the Australian Government.[13]

Hard on the heels of the Whitlam visit came the United Nations visiting mission to report on Australia's fulfilment of its obligations to the Trust Territory of

New Guinea. This examination and report occurred
every third year. The mission comprised representatives
of four countries, some of whom might be expected to
be sympathetic, and some critical but not hostile. The
1971 mission was led by Sir Denis Allen of the United
Kingdom, supported by Paul Blanc of France, Adnan
Raouf of Iraq and C.E. Wyse of Sierra Leone. The
Whitlam group left on 17 January and the UN visiting
mission arrived on 24 January. On the assumption that
idle hands might be mischievous we had arranged a
demanding itinerary. For instance the programme for
24 February in the Highlands Districts was:

> Visited Territory malarial school
> Visited Chimbu coffee co-operative
> Departed Kundiawa for Wandi by vehicle
> Public meeting
> Inspected Kerowagi High School
> Meeting with students of Kerowagi and Kandiu High
> Schools
> En route to Kundiawa visit Mr Danga Mondo's agri-
> cultural block
> Return Kundiawa

The report of the mission recorded the rigours endured:

> During its tour, the Mission held fifty meetings and
> discussions with members of local government councils
> and with the general public. It also held thirteen
> meetings with representative groups, organizations and
> associations. It visited twenty-four educational insti-
> tutions and held discussions with students. It also in-
> spected hospitals and medical centres, and thirty-four
> other institutions, including manufacturing and indus-
> trial establishments, co-operative societies, agricultural
> projects and processing plants. It also held many
> meetings with administrative officials in the various
> districts. Informal discussions were held with in-
> dividuals in all walks of life on numerous occasions.[14]

All this took place in the space of forty days, only three

of which were free from engagements. In that time they had travelled 16,824 kilometres within Papua New Guinea by land, sea and air.

The mission's recommendations followed pretty closely what we were doing, or trying to do. The central recommendations were numbers 469, 472, 497 and 499.

469. The lack of political parties with a solid nation-wide base is a source of weakness in the House of Assembly; consideration should be given to possible means of encouraging existing parties to establish a truly national organization (paras. 286–289).

472. Localization of the public service needs a new impetus, especially in the Division of District Administration; there is an urgent need to establish a clear programme for retention of experienced expatriate officers with special skills and for adequate compensation of those displaced; special attention needs to be paid to conditions of service of local officers, especially in the field of housing (paras. 299–306).

E. *Future of the Territory*
497. The Mission endorses the findings of the Select Committee on Constitutional Development; in particular it agrees with the Committee that since the rate of political development is accelerating there may be a majority demand for internal self-government before the end of the 1972–1976 House of Assembly; and that, in consequence, the development of the Territory should be geared to preparing it for self-government during the life of the next House (para. 460).

499. While the chief responsibility for setting a date for independence should rest with the government of a self-governing Papua New Guinea, the Mission believes that it would be both prudent and realistic to assume for planning purposes that independence will be achieved during the life of the Fourth House of Assembly (para. 463).

The mission then visited Canberra to discuss its

findings with the Minister for External Territories, C.E. Barnes, who had outlined to the Prime Minister the rather restrained lines he proposed to take with the mission. Gorton responded by urging a more positive approach to devolution.

> I believe that we should, as far as possible, move with any foreshortening of the independence timescale. I think that it is important both in the discussions with the UN Mission and the debate in the Territory House of Assembly to avoid giving any impression that the Government is attempting to delay the achievement of internal self-government. In fact, the existence of some of the problems which you have raised to early self-government, such as the quality of leadership, the quality of executive support and the law and order capacity could well be interpreted by our critics as being of our own making. Under these circumstances I believe it would be advisable to avoid nominating time-scales for the retention of certain powers such as retaining responsibility for the public service and the Magistracy until 1975. I think that the intermediate step of promoting indigene participation in all aspects of government should be accelerated. In particular, if the police officer component is largely expatriate and not well trained, increased, emphasis should be placed on training programmes for indigenous officers.[16]

These events moved public opinion forward, but it now required the co-operation of the House of Assembly to embrace and adopt this accelerated approach. In this context the report of the House of Assembly's Select Committee on Constitutional Development and its treatment by the House would dictate how rapidly we could proceed. The Select Committee had been established in June 1969 on the motion of Paulus Arek, an ambitious ex-teacher, who saw it as a means of projecting himself into political prominence. At that time the possibility of such a committee accelerating the pace of political development was disturbing to the Minister and his Canberra department and we official members were briefed to delay the presentation of the motion. Arek finally presented it at the March meeting in 1969 but it was not debated until the following meeting in June, by which time it had been decided that the officials should adopt a "hands off" position. "The Administration considers that a decision to establish a constitutional committee now, or to defer such an establishment till later, is essentially a matter for the elected members to take and we do not consider that it is a decision in which official members should intervene."[17]

There was general support for the proposal; of the twenty-two speakers only four were in opposition. Pita Lus was the most outspoken; "This man [Leahy] said that we must wait, didn't he? If we do this it will be after we die that independence comes."[18] However, most speakers, with a wary eye on the electorate, were careful to point out that independence, or even self-government, was not what the motion was all about. Of the four who opposed, Leahy suggested delay for a year or so, while the others in opposition were conservative highlanders whose opposition to political progress was embedded in their system of beliefs. Tei Abal faithfully reflected the views of the Minister for External Territories: "We must have a sound economic background and be able to support political change."[19] However the House accepted the proposal without a division and set up a committee of fourteen with Arek as Chairman and myself as his Deputy. The Committee's membership ensured that radical proposals would be unlikely, but it did contain leading progressives; Michael Somare, Ebia Olewale, Oala Oala Rarua and Paulus Arek. In the period prior to the Gorton visit the official members (Geoff Littler and I) were expected to use our best endeavours to restrain the committee from adventurous proposals. In part, our briefing paper, prepared in the Department of External Territories read: "Official members' general posture would be to seed ideas, very often through Leahy or the Ministerial Members on the Committee. They would, however, make sure that they were briefed on the Government's position so that elected members did not think that the Government would agree to something that it would be unlikely to agree to."[20]

The changed circumstances after July 1970 evoked a very different response from the Department of External Territories. All was eagerness to coax forthcoming recommendations from the Select Committee — to extract a commitment to a date for self-government, and to obtain proposals for increased local responsibility. As the Select Committee moved towards its final recommendations I wrote a personal note to its executive officer, Allan Kerr (seconded from External Territories):

> Opinion within your Department is moving towards a timetable appropriate for self-government and I believe that the Minister is beginning to change his mind. However, as you know, both the Minister and the Prime Minister are very publicly committed to a "no timetable" approach. I think that they would like to get off this hook but could only do so by accepting a recommendation of the Select Committee along those lines.[21]

The Select Committee, however, was cautious, and conscious of the need for recommendations that would be acceptable to a large majority of the House, still decidedly conservative in its attitude towards self-government. The Select Committee felt that a precise target date would be unacceptable, even if its members could agree about it. The Select Committee's report was presented to the House on 4 March 1971.[22]

The key recommendation went some way towards

meeting the wishes of Canberra. Arek, introducing the report, said "Your committee therefore recommends that the development of the territory be geared to preparing the country for internal self-government during the life of the next House of Assembly."[23] This meant during the period 1972–76, but the Select Committee had shied away from setting a firm target date. In brief, the central recommendations were:

1. That there should only be one chamber (Barnes had fancied the idea of a chamber of review).
2. That House membership be increased to one hundred elected members, eighty-two from open electorates and eighteen from regional electorates. In addition, provision should be made for three nominated members if the House so wished and that there should be four nominated official members.
3. The AEC should comprise the Administrator as Chairman, ten Ministers and three of the official members of the House of Assembly.
4. That, following the nomination of the Ministers by the Ministerial Nominations Committee composed of seven members of the House, the Ministers should choose one of their number to be the Deputy Chairman of the AEC, which choice should be approved by the House of Assembly.

This procedure for choosing Ministers had been instituted in the second House of Assembly. It was rather a complicated process. The House elected the members of the ministerial nominations committee which then, in consultation with the Administrator, agreed upon a ministerial list. The Committee then presented the list to the House for approval and finally they were formally appointed by the Minister for External Territories. Almost everyone had a hand in it.

There was wide support for the recommendations in

the report but some of the conservatives felt obliged to object to the proposal concerning the date for self-government. Tei Abal was their spokesman:

> There is one part we, the Compass Party, reject and that is the suggestion that self-government will be due in the period between 1972 and 1976. We consider that even within that period we will not be ready for it. The Compass Party feels that between 1976 and 1980 may be the appropriate period to achieve self-government.[24]

However no move was made to amend this section of the report, members confining themselves to the rather more cosmetic areas.

The Select Committee found one of its tasks particularly difficult, and that was to reach agreement on a suitable name, a crest, a flag and a national anthem for the country. These matters had been first broached by John Guise in 1965 when he was Chairman of the Constitutional Commitee of the first House of Assembly but his efforts had been firmly discouraged by fiat from the Department of External Territories which considered that such symbols might accelerate political development. But four years later this prohibition no longer pertained. It was hoped that these symbols would help to develop a national consciousness, a sentiment now approved in high places given the problems arising from separatist movements in various parts of the country. A section of the report read:

> Your committee recognizes that a unified country and people is of the utmost importance in the move forward to internal self-government and later to independence, and during the Committee tours many people called for unity in Papua and New Guinea. One name, one flag and crest will help to create a feeling of national identity for our nation.[25]

There was widespread interest in these matters and the Select Committee was inundated with suggestions and sketches. Over opposition from Papuan members of the Select Committee the name "Niugini" was recommended. Niugini has obvious Pidgin origins but it was also alleged that, in part, it meant "a stand of coconuts" in Motu, a language of the Papuan coast. Almost all suggestions for a crest and a flag featured a bird of paradise and this was incorporated in the ultimate recommendations for both these symbols, though the decision on a flag was very much a last-minute job. No national anthem came from the many suggested, though the band master of the Police Band did his best to promote a composition of his own by including it every time that the band performed in public.

It was to these features of the report that members directed a good deal of their oratory. The main recommendations did not go unchallenged, but the fact that the Select Committee included members from both the conservative and progressive sides of the House meant that members speaking critically of the political development proposed were doing little more than posturing. Substantive amendments were directed only at the peripheral elements of the report.

Paliau Maloat moved to abolish regional electorates, the undisclosed reason being that expatriates had considerable advantage in contesting seats due to their greater mobility and the fact that clan support was of less significance over a much larger area (eleven of the fifteen regional electorates were held by expatriates). The amendment was soundly defeated forty-seven to seventeen, but it might be noted that in the next election only four of the eighteen regional seats were won by expatriates. Tei Abal moved to defer a decision on a flag and managed to get a tied vote, but the Speaker, dutifully following Westminster practice, and his own inclinations, cast the decisive negative vote against the amendment. Toua Kapena moved to reject the name

"Niugini" and, after a lengthy debate which wore everybody down, Kapena won his point without a division at 11.15 p.m. Immediately afterwards, the House adopted the report as amended. A few days later Percy Chatterton moved that the House approve the name Papua New Guinea for the country, which the House quickly accepted, only one other member speaking on the motion.[26] The Territory of Papua and New Guinea suffered only minor changes and became Papua New Guinea.

There was a considerable sense of relief both in Canberra and Port Moresby for we could now see our way clear to prepare for self-government somewhere between 1972 and 1976. Given the expectation that the 1972 elections would produce a conservative majority I felt that 1975 might be a realistic target, but in any case we proceeded to assemble a team comprising officers from both External Territories and the Administration to plan transition.

On 1 July a *Papua New Guinea Government Gazette Extraordinary* was issued which contained a coloured picture of our new flag and a sketch of our new emblem. It also included a section setting out our new name though people had to study it pretty hard to find any differences from the old one. The gazette also nominated 15 September as National Day. I wrote a special message for the gazette:

> During its June meeting the House of Assembly passed the National Identity Bill establishing a national name, a flag and an emblem for this country . . . These things — a name, a flag and an emblem — are the symbols of a nation, but in themselves they cannot create a nation. A nation is created by people and by those people feeling that they belong together. It is created by people with common aspirations and people who will work together to achieve those aspirations.
> All of these may not yet be present in Papua New

Guinea but I believe that they will grow; a feeling of unity will grow until not only do we have the outward symbols of nationhood but we are truly one people.[27]

In September we duly celebrated our National Day in style at centres throughout the country. In Port Moresby there was a large and happy gathering, where we raised our new flag amid great acclamation, the honour being given to the young schoolgirl Susan Karike who had submitted the chosen design. As usual, I was required to make a speech — I thought it rather good — and I hope that you will bear with two extracts from it:

> We have grown as a nation at prodigious speed. Do you remember Papua New Guinea and its people as they were just ten years ago? Do you remember our road system in 1961? Do you remember how many high schools we had then? Only five years ago we began our university. Seven years ago our House of Assembly had its first meeting. One year ago the Select Committee on Constitutional Development recommended that we should prepare for self-government between 1972 and 1976. . . .
> Some, perhaps many, in Papua New Guinea do not understand what is happening. They are still not part of it and shrink from the unknown. Those who do understand, those who feel pride in achievement, pride in being a member of a new nation must not forget and leave behind those who do not. Our greatest task — your greatest task — is one of communication, understanding and sympathy. It is not sufficient to take a fraction of the people into nationhood — we must take all of them.[28]

The Australian Government had, of course, already accepted the recommendations. On 27 April Barnes made a statement in the House of Representatives:

> I wish to inform the House that the Government has accepted the recommendations of the Papua New Guinea House of Assembly. . . . This attitude [the

1972–1976 target] accords with the Government's policies of encouraging progress towards internal self-government and of looking to the elected members of the House of Assembly to represent the ·wishes of the majority of the people in such matters as the pace and nature of constitutional development.[29]

This seems to be a suitable quote with which to conclude this chapter.

NOTES

1. Johnson broadcast, reprinted in *The Australian*, 26 December 1970.
2. The Final Report of the Select Committee on Constitutional Development, P.N.G., House of Assembly Debates (HAD), vol. I, no. 13, p. 2340.
3. At present Lokoloko is Governor-General of Papua New Guinea.
4. Letter, Administrator to Minister, 9 January 1971, PP.
5. Personal recollection, Ken McKinnon.
6. Administrator to Minister, op. cit.
7. "I think you are not men but boys."
8. Press statement made by Whitlam on leaving Papua New Guinea, 17 January 1971, PP.
9. Circular instruction to District Commissioners, 18 December 1970, PP.
10. *The Canberra Times*, 11 January 1971.
11. Whitlam press statement, op. cit.
12. Ibid.
13. Letter, Johnson to Hay, 19 January 1971, PP.
14. Report of the UN Visiting Mission to the Trust Territory of New Guinea 1971 Trusteeship Council, official records, 38th Session.
15. Ibid.
16. Gorton to Barnes, 22 January 1971, PP.
17. P.N.G., HAD, vol. II, no. 5, p. 1144, statement by Johnson.
18. Ibid, p. 1143 (Lus).
19. Ibid, p. 1147.
20. External Territories briefing paper, July 1969, PP.
21. Johnson to Kerr, 15 January 1971, PP.
22. P.N.G., HAD, vol. II, no. 13, p. 3804.
23. Ibid, p. 3805.
24. Ibid, p. 3884.
25. Ibid, p. 3804.
26. Ibid, p. 4009.

27. *Papua New Guinea Government Gazette Extraordinary*, Port Moresby, 1 July 1971; message in English, Pidgin and Motu.
28. Copy among personal papers.
29. *Selected Policy Statements, Papua New Guinea 1970–71*, AGPS, Canberra.

5

1971

During 1971 national political development seemed to be moving in the right direction but there were a myriad other preoccupations in the course of that year. I count it as the busiest year of my life.

The job of Administrator is hard to define. In theory his powers are strictly limited, like those of any other public servant. His activities are bound by ministerial direction, almost invariably conveyed to him through the Australian Department of External Territories. Given the range of decisions to be made, only a Minister with long experience and vast industry such as Paul Hasluck, could be confident of managing effectively both his Department and his distant satrapy centred in Port Moresby. With the departure of Hasluck at the end of 1963 there was a power vacuum which was only partly filled by his successor, C.E. Barnes, who was in his first Ministry, and, at that, one far removed from his past experience and his personal interests. C.E. Barnes was more heavily dependent on the advice of his public servants than his predecessor, and in this those on the spot in Canberra enjoyed considerable advantages over their opposite numbers in Port Moresby. It should be noted that Australians in the Papua New

Guinea service were employed and paid by the Papua New Guinea Administration and not by the Australian Government. They were a distinct and separate body from the Australian Public Service. Their loyalty was owed directly to the Administrator.

The communications from External Territories in Canberra to Port Moresby in the name of the Minister, could be, and frequently were, couched as directions, their execution mandatory. Advice and recommendations to the Minister from Port Moresby were sent almost invariably via the Department of External Territories, though the Administrator could communicate directly with the Minister if he wished. But all communications underwent the scrutiny of officers of the Department and their advice on the matters raised was added to that tendered from Port Moresby. There were occasions when recommendations from Port Moresby did not get as far as the Minister's desk.

However, the Administrator was not entirely toothless in this territorial battle. He was the man on the spot; if he persisted, his advice to the Minister could not be ignored or overridden. He could, and did, take initiatives on many things without reference to Canberra, though such actions were frequently challenged by the Department. He could delay the implementation of directions with which he did not agree by interminable procrastination. He could enlist local opinion for or against particular projects; critics might say he could "orchestrate" it. In particular, an alliance between the Administrator and the House of Assembly was a high card to play. Further, in Papua New Guinea the Administrator enjoyed high status and prestige; activities which did not have his support were unlikely to succeed.

For the Department of External Territories, Australian interests were the primary consideration, while for the Papua New Guinea Administration the welfare of Papua New Guinea was paramount, so that, on many issues, disagreement was inevitable. When those interests coincided there was still room for differences on how best to achieve the agreed ends. From 1964 until 1970, the principle of confrontation applied. Let there be a war of ideas and methods, with the strongest surviving. From 1964 until 1966 the principal protagonists were Smith, the Secretary Department of External Territories, in Canberra and Gunther, the Assistant Administrator, in Port Moresby, with the Administrator, Cleland, somewhat above the battle. From 1967 until 1970 Smith and Hay were in the ring, I judge with the points going to Smith until the final round, when Smith was knocked out and supplanted as Secretary of the Department by Hay. From 1970 onwards Hay and I tried the co-operative approach and I think that we would both agree that it worked pretty well, though it must be said that by that time many of the points of difference between the two administrations had been eliminated by the Australian Government's decision to speed Papua New Guinea to independence and to pass as much of the burden of decision making to Papua New Guinean Ministers as they were prepared to take. This latter policy shift sharply increased the Administrator's influence, at least at first, as those Ministers relied heavily upon the Administrator and their Papua New Guinea departmental officers for advice and guidance.

What actually were the duties and responsibilities of the Administrator after July 1970, when Ministerial Members had extensive powers delegated to them? First of all, he was the representative of the Australian Government and, in the absence of Australian Ministers, spoke for that government in Papua New Guinea. He was responsible for ensuring the implementation of Australian policies regarding Papua New Guinea and, of course, for advising the Australian Government on appropriate policies to pursue. Although many powers had now been devolved upon Papua New Guinean Ministers, they were powers delegated by the Administrator and, as Chairman of the Administrator's Executive Council, which was in effect the Cabinet of Papua New Guinea and the focal point for the exercise of those powers, the Administrator had a powerful voice, if he chose to exercise it, in the policy decisions arrived at in the AEC.

He was the bridge between the Australian Government and the embryonic Papua New Guinea Government and the public servants who served it. Where powers had not been delegated, departmental heads were directly responsible to the Administrator, for instance district administration, law, security, intelligence and police. The Administrator was also an informal court of appeal when Ministers of Papua New Guinea and their departmental heads were in serious disagreement.

As the titular head of the Papua New Guinea Government the Administrator had many statutory functions to perform. In the course of every week his signature legitimized the transactions of many government departments and agencies. Until the middle of 1972 he was the principal source of official information to the media, through a weekly press conference. He was called upon to make speeches on all sorts of occasions; at agricultural shows, graduation ceremonies, fund raisings, book launchings and so on, to open conferences, bridges, new buildings, training courses and everything else that could be opened. The Administrator's office was usually the first port of call for official visitors and he was expected to provide information and sustenance for many of them. If the

visitors were of sufficient eminence they were house-
guests. Among these guests I recall with pleasure the
Queen, Prince Philip, Princess Anne and Captain
Philips, Sir Paul Hasluck, by then Governor-General,
Robert Macnamara of the World Bank, David Trench,
then Governor of Hong Kong, Gough and Margaret
Whitlam, Morrice James the British High Commissioner, Adam Malik, then Indonesia's Foreign Minister,
Peggy van Pragh of the Australian Ballet, and, of
course, pretty well all of the Australian Ministers of the
day, often with their wives. A fairly typical day recorded in my diary follows:

Thursday August 26 1971

8.00   Australian businessmen (site for tourist develop-
       ment)
9.00   Press conference
10.00 Oil company executives (Esso)
11.00 New town development inspection of possible
       sites for High Court, foreign embassies,
       Australian High Commission
1.30   Nauwi Sauinambi (MHA for Ambunti Yangoru)
2.45   Chief of General Staff (General Brogan)
3.30   First Asst Sec. DET: Gutman — economic
       development
4.00   Professor Salisbury (Gazelle Report)
6.00   Reception Government House. Local Govern-
       ment Association
8.15   ABC Concert at UPNG

Until there was wide general acceptance of indigenous political leaders, the Administrator was the
visible presence of the Government and was obliged to
be seen and heard throughout the country. He had to
turn up at trouble spots, such as in the Gazelle and in
Bougainville, he had to be present to allay anxieties of

the highlanders and to reassure people that Australian assistance would continue after self-government, to encourage acceptance of Papua New Guinea Government decisions and to listen to and try to resolve grievances (there were always plenty of them). I would usually return to Port Moresby with a notebook full of "follow-ups". Such excursions were not all hard labour. I found Papua New Guinea such a beautiful country that travelling, whether by canoe, Land-rover, trawler or on foot, was a continuous pleasure. The warmly-hospitable people were as varied as their environments, from the swamps and mosquitoes of the Fly River to the remote coral atolls, from the deep valleys and rugged mountains of the Western and Southern Highlands District to the fruitful plains of the Markham valley, from the lush growth on the volcanic ash of New Britain to the harsh savannah around Port Moresby.

David Hay had begun the practice of holding AEC meetings at intervals at different centres in Papua New Guinea, which I maintained. It gave the people a chance to see their political leaders en masse and for those leaders to be exposed to the problems of areas which otherwise they might never have visited.

Public relations was an on-going affair but a major preoccupation during 1971 was the continuing dissatisfaction of the people of Bougainville with their lot within Papua New Guinea, amounting to outright calls for secession. There was, as well, a rising tide of discontent among Papuans, who saw what they regarded as their special status with respect to Australia threatened by the approach of self-government. Separation became a bogy. Gough Whitlam raised the issue in an address at Monash University. "The most worrying political problem in Papua New Guinea at the moment is the growth of separatism. There can be nothing more destructive, more weakening or more self-defeating."[1]

The people of Bougainville had never felt particularly closely associated with the rest of Papua New Guinea. Their kinship ties were with the people of the island of Guadalcanal in the Solomon Islands (then under British suzerainty as the British Solomon Islands Protectorate). The people of Bougainville were distinctly different in appearance from any of their fellow citizens in Papua New Guinea and had always felt that they had been neglected by the central government — a not unjustifiable grievance. The advent of a huge copper mine and the local resistance to its establishment had reinforced those feelings until secession was being widely canvassed and we anticipated that secession advocates would probably win all the Bougainville seats at the next election, despite the incongruity of a secessionist becoming a part of a national parliament. During a brief visit to Bougainville, John Gorton had flown a kite about regionalism through the devolution of powers to groupings of local government councils, hoping to steal some thunder from the outright secessionists. I had taken up the same theme in an address to the annual meeting of the Local Government Association by suggesting that adjacent councils should pool their resources and act in common in development plans, perhaps ultimately forming a third or intermediate level of government. But the prime target of these proposals, Bougainville, remained unmoved. The people of Bougainville stayed on the brink but hesitated to jump, and it was thought unlikely that they would take any positive action until they had considered their status in an independent Papua New Guinea.

The Papuan problem was different — they were not seeking to secede but to protect their status and to get a better share of the cake. They were afraid that in a self-governing Papua New Guinea they would be overwhelmed by the more numerous New Guineans, and their interests set aside. Yano Belo from the electorate of Kagua in the Southern Highlands[2] spoke for his fellow Papuans.

> I would like to reiterate that the Administration falls short in the assistance it gives us compared to that rendered to other areas. . . . Like other Papuan areas we get nothing. There are areas . . . which the Administration has been in contact with for about a hundred years but in terms of development these areas are way behind. There are no modern facilities, no roads and not enough schools. We have virtually nothing.[3]

Certainly development projects in the Papuan Districts (Central, Milne Bay, Northern, Western, Gulf, Southern Highlands) were limited, but principally because of their meagre exploitable resources and the difficult terrain; swamps in the coastal areas, precipitous mountains inland and a scatter of innumerable islands in the east. Except in the valleys of the Southern Highlands District, population was sparse. Even so, there were some small groups hidden away among the swamps who had only rarely been contacted from the outside. At least one such small group still resorted to cannibalism and this resulted in the arrest and detention of seven men who had stolen a corpse from neighbours and eaten it. When, after some months of detention, they were brought to trial, the judge released them unconvicted. The press, alert for a headline, asked me if I proposed to do anything further to eliminate the practice; the transcript notes that I replied flippantly "No, but at least they will now have a taste for rice and bully beef."[4]

Papua rumbled with discontent, and I deemed it necessary for the Australian Government to set out, in clear terms, its position in respect to Papua. Accordingly I was authorized to make a statement.

I am authorized by the Minister for External Territories, Mr C.E. Barnes, to re-affirm that it is the policy of the Australian Government to advance Papua New Guinea to internal self-government and independence as a united country. In particular I am authorized to say that, in the Government's view, there is no ground for any people of Papua New Guinea to expect, as self-government and independence approach, that their present legal status will lead to any difference in their treatment by the Australian Government or the Administration, or in their rights. In practice the difference of legal status between the inhabitants of Papua on the one hand and New Guinea on the other has been of little consequence since the approval by the United Nations of the administrative union in 1947. The Government sees no other long term course for Papua New Guinea than one directed towards internal self-government and independence for the country as a whole.[5]

This did little to calm the Papuans, and Bert Counsel, an Australian, long resident in Papua, and the member for the Gulf/Western District, initiated a debate in the House of Assembly on the "political welfare of the Papuan People"[6] and followed it up with a motion "that this House requests the Australian Government not to alter the existing status and rights of Papua and Papuans without the express approval of the Papuan people or their elected representatives."[7] Momei Pangial, from Mendi in the Southern Highlands, then chipped in to move "that the House requests the Australian Government to appoint a Commonwealth Parliamentary committee comprising representatives of all political parties to make an early visit to Papua to determine the wishes of the Papuan people and to learn of their concern at first hand."[8]

Counsel's motion was passed thirty to twenty-five, the majority achieved by an alliance of all Papuan members with the Pangu Pati and the newly developed

People's Progress Party. Politics makes for strange bed
fellows as "Pangu" stood for "Papua and New Guinea
Union". A few days later, Momei's motion was passed
without a division.

Australians (in Australia) were outraged. The
Melbourne *Age* of 3 June 1971 fulminated:

> By a narrow vote in the Port Moresby House of
> Assembly the elected Territory parliament has set back
> the plans for self-government enthusiastically adopted
> by the Australian Government with the full approval of
> the Opposition and the whole-hearted backing of the
> United Nations. Responsibility and progress have been
> thrown out of the window by an angry and confused
> bunch of black and white legislators moved by a weird
> complex of fears for the future and antipathies inherited
> from the past.

In fact it was nothing of the sort. The House of
Assembly members were always indulgently disposed
towards "motions" or "resolutions" which dominated
debate in most sittings. Members recognized that they
were an expression of opinion and were never too upset
if they were advised of a polite negative via a letter to
the Speaker from the Administrator. In the case of the
Papuan resolution, so much dust had been stirred up
that it was obvious that we would have to make a
placatory gesture, but continued progress towards self-
government was never in doubt.

The Papuan members recognized that the implementation of the resolutions was unlikely, but having
got majority support for them, they then decided to
send a delegation of Papuan Ministers' to Canberra to
see the Prime Minister and other Ministers to enlist
sympathy for their disadvantages as they saw them. In
view of the projected visit I wrote to the Department,
on 5 October 1971; "The Papuan Ministers will suffer a
great deal of criticism if they do not bring back some

concessions." At the November meeting of the House, Oala Rarua made the best of the rather meagre results of the expedition.

> The delegation expressed general satisfaction with the outcome of its discussions with the Minister for External Territories. It is felt that the Minister is now very much more aware of the importance that Papuans place on the development of Papua.
>
> The Minister has undertaken to engage an independent consultant to make a study for the less developed areas of Papua New Guinea with a view to preparing development programmes for those areas.[10]

The Minister had stuck to his guns and refused to treat Papua as a special problem but had made a concession which might bear some fruit in the future.

At any rate the push by the Papuans for a protected corner in the Australian sun produced a movement which developed from a pressure group into a political party — Papua Besena, which translates broadly into "the Papua family". The originator was a Papuan woman, Josephine Abaijah, who, assisted by some skilful propaganda, became a prominent figure in the political spectrum and the first woman to be elected to the House of Assembly in the 1972 elections.

At the end of the year, I endeavoured to encapsulate the situation in both Papua and Bougainville in this communication to the Minister:

> Without discounting the fact that the pre-war administration in Papua had developed some sense of Papuan unity, the clamour of the Papuans was largely generated by hopes of obtaining some economic advantages. They wanted a greater share of the national resources diverted to their districts and they clung to the possibility that their nominal Australian citizenship might be a further bargaining point. . . . Ultimately all of the more responsible Papuan leaders accepted the goal of national unity.

Bougainville, however, is and will remain genuinely secessionist. At present the strength of the movement is in the centre and the south with the north speaking for unity, but this is rather more an indication of internal political rivalries than fundamentally opposed feelings. Almost all of the people of Bougainville are basically secessionist and at this point it is hard to see what courses of action are likely to change them. It is not a problem which causes much administrative difficulty now, but most certainly it is a grave problem for the future.[11]

Events in Bougainville stimulated fissiparous attitudes in many different parts of Papua New Guinea, and when the independent government of Papua New Guinea later deemed it necessary to extend a degree of autonomy to Bougainville it had little choice but to do it elsewhere. Clearly, for good or ill, Bougainville precipitated provincial government in Papua New Guinea.

The year 1971 was a very active one on the economic front; specifically in a drive to expand indigenous participation in economic pursuits. Efforts faced two ways — first, to promote greater involvement in small business and rural production, and second, to obtain a share in the ownership of the big concerns. One of the difficulties faced by Papua New Guineans seeking loans was that Papua New Guinea banks were branches of Australian banks and played the game by Australian rules, which meant that borrowers had to have a secure title to land or other security before money could be advanced. Many Papua New Guineans had customary rights to use land or had assets that were held in common with kin but they could not meet the bank's criteria for a loan. Two ways to remedy this were tried. The obvious way was to speed up and simplify the conversion of land from group ownership to individual freehold title. The other way was to set up a Papua New Guinea bank to operate under a different set of rules. This second alternative had been accomplished as early as 1967 when the Papua New Guinea Development Bank was established, and this had gone some way towards giving Papua New Guineans access to capital. At the official opening of the bank the Minister (Barnes) had said "the Development Bank will especially serve the small producer and the small businessman. In making loans it will look primarily at the borrower's financial prospects rather than the value of the security he can offer."[12]

Land conversion was a much greater problem. A number of attempts were made to simplify the process and to speed up the conversion of community-held land to individual title. We brought the legislation to the brink several times but members of the House always baulked, or so bowdlerized the legislation as to make it unworkable. Of course the error was ours — we were trying to fit Papua New Guinea society into an Australian mould, rather than adjusting our own procedures to meet the mores of the indigenous society. All of our parliamentarians recognized that fiddling with land ownership would be suicidal, politically.

Nevertheless in 1971 we tried again. Our renewed effort had, in fact, been years in the making, and this time we went far afield for our model. A number of our politicians had visited Kenya, and had been impressed by its politicians and interested in its land laws. As early as 1969 we commissioned a Kenyan Englishman, Rowton Simpson, to advise us on reform of our land laws, had followed that up with a visit to Kenya by a technical committee and then set out to work up the legislation. We had taken the greatest care to publicize what we were doing and to invite discussion and debate both within the House of Assembly and outside it on a number of occasions, yet when the Bills (four of them) were produced there was an immediate outcry. The debate was not well informed, and even usually reliable supporters were prepared to desert us. Toua Kapena, the Ministerial Member for Labour, made a contribution to the debate which was symptomatic of unreasoning opposition: "When the British Government first landed in this country, it hoisted its flag in my village. At that time it made a proclamation to protect our land. All the old people did not know the importance of the land at that time. I will not support this Bill."[13] True, the Bills were complex, but opposition to them was due to a refusal to face up to decisions about land holding. We gave up and withdrew the Bills hoping that they might be re-introduced later, but mentally listing them as a problem for an independent government.

In the matter of increasing the participation of Papua New Guineans in economic ventures or "wok bisnis"[14] a new Department had been created — Business Development, headed by a Papua New Guinean, Paulias Matane, whose specific function was to encourage and assist Papua New Guineans to set up businesses and get going, and this implied a degree of exclusion of expatriates from small business operations. Concurrently, we set about restricting the entry to the country of expatriates with low level skills, if they came to get jobs, and gradually to expand the list of exclusions as indigenes with appropriate skills became available. I had already taken up the matter of the expatriate sector assisting the development of indigenous businessmen in a speech at the opening of the Morobe District Agricultural Show. My speech included a paragraph which the white populace of Lae found indigestible, though Australian businessmen in both Port Moresby and Rabaul asked for suggestions as to how they could assist.

Let me be quite explicit. I am not advocating selfless altruism for expatriate businessmen but I am advocating measures whereby mutual confidence and respect can be developed between Papua New Guineans and expatriates. This can only be based on equality. There is no long term security for anyone in the indefinite continuation of the vast gap between expatriate and Papua New Guinean, and that gap must be bridged. It is idle to talk of a multiracial society unless this is a society whose members can mingle on equal terms. That society must ensure that its members have the means to mingle on equal terms.[15]

Meanwhile we had extended to local government councils the power to refuse an application for a new trade store licence if refusal was necessary to protect a Papua New Guinean trading enterprise within the council area.

The coping stone of our administrative actions was the establishment of the Investment Corporation. We had already adopted a policy of requiring a government shareholding in particular industries about to be established. We had acquired a twenty per cent share in the Bougainville Copper Mine and we had fifty per cent of a large oil palm venture in West New Britain, consisting of a big nucleus estate with factory, surrounded by small holders selling their produce to the factory for processing. Now we planned to systematize it through a corporation which would take up equity on behalf of Papua New Guinea in ventures which promised to be profitable. These would be held in trust and could be disposed of at a later date to citizens who had become sufficiently affluent to acquire shares in their own right. Bougainville Copper had already reserved shares for local residents and a good many Papua New Guineans held small parcels of shares in the copper mine in addition to the Papua New Guinea Government's holding of twenty percent. Papua New Guineans' participation in the cash economy was still very small, but at least the opportunities had expanded somewhat and some measures of positive discrimination had been cautiously implemented.

But in terms of discriminating in favour of Papua New Guineans in the Public Service, I was still battling it out with the Public Service Board whose rigidity was in part due to the difficulty in getting Australian Government approval of a suitable compensation scheme for displaced expatriates. The Employment Security Scheme (ESS) was almost the sole topic of conversation among white public servants. In irritation, I wrote to David Hay in January 1971:

> I must say that the more one looks at the development of self-government here, the more essential it becomes to ally the Public Service Board in some clear constitutional way with the emerging Papua New Guinea Government. The continued separation of the Public Service Board negates all attempts at rational planning, making it completely dependent on the thorough-going co-operation of the Public Service Board, which cannot always be guaranteed.[16]

I have earlier referred to the lack of communication between the Public Service Board and myself, as Administrator and Chairman of the AEC. Among other things, it led to the confrontation between the House of Assembly and the Public Service Board over the latter's unilateral decision to change the name of the Administrative College and to call it the Public Service Training Institute. As far as I can guess the change was little more than an assertion of the Public Service Board's independence from the Administration, the Papua New Guinea Ministers and the House of Assembly. Of course it lay within the competence of the Board to change the name of the institution which served its own training purposes, and of course the

House of Assembly had no mandate to interfere, but the action was so clearly a provocative challenge that it invited a riposte. Even considered calmly ten years later, I think that the Public Service Board's action was extremely foolish and insensitive.

The Board did not surrender easily. It made strenuous attempts to persuade the Minister to veto the legislation approved by the House which revoked the name change. There was a voluble exchange of views orally and by letter. The AEC recommended strongly against the use of veto powers and I insisted on going to Canberra personally to argue the Council's case to the Minister should he be inclined to embrace the veto argument. A veto on this matter would assuredly have caused a tremendous uproar in Papua New Guinea. Eventually the Minister agreed with us, and the Public Service Training Institute once more became the Administrative College. At about the same time we had a new Chairman of the Board, Sere Pitoi, the first Papua New Guinean Chairman, and occupying one of the two most senior public service positions in the country, excluding that of Administrator.[17]

Meanwhile we continued to experience the greatest difficulty in moving Papua New Guineans into executive posts because of the Public Service appeal provisions available to unsuccessful applicants for promotion. Unless preference was exercised in favour of indigenous public servants, as it could be under Section 49 of the Public Service Ordinance, Papuan New Guinean appointees were knocked over like ninepins by better qualified and more experienced expatriate appellants. The Director of Education, Ken McKinnon, outlined the dismal record in a minute to me: "Thus the record shows that seven — seven of the most worthwhile of our local officers — have all lost promotion in the last three months! The manner of their losing is such that I no longer have any confidence that a local officer can get through the system no matter how good he is."[18] In the Department of District Administration, there were similar problems, as four of five promotions of indigenous officers to the post of District Officer were negated on the appeals of expatriates.

I met with the reconstituted Public Service Board, under its new Chairman, in July of 1971, to try to resolve half of the problem by providing both specialized training and work experience for promising indigenous officers, and then pushing them into selected senior posts. My own minutes of the meeting record: "The Public Service Board and the Administrator agree as to the urgency of having a group of men ready to fill a significant proportion of the positions at Class eleven and above, including Departmental Heads, within a very short space of time. It is necessary to have some of these posts filled within the year and from then onwards the pace should accelerate."[19] We were, of course, victims of our own folly, in having imported the entire apparatus of the Australian Public Service system, including an appeals procedure that had the capacity to frustrate essential policy decisions. But, as I have previously indicated, something had to be done to provide protection for those expatriate officers, permanent members of the Papua New Guinea Public Service, who would be displaced. Several attempts had been made to put together a suitable compensation scheme for loss of career but all of these broke upon the rock of Australian Treasury resistance to putting up the cash.

Meanwhile, it had been possible to move some Papua New Guineans up the scale by other devices and subterfuges. One was to create senior advisory positions in departments into which we would move expatriate officers sideways and then avoid appeals against indigenous replacements in the original position by making only temporary appointments which were non-appealable. It must be said that our expatriate officers appreciated the problem, and were co-operative, but understandably enough they had their own interests to protect, and many of them who may have had twenty or more years service in Papua New Guinea were apprehensive about their prospects for employment in Australia at age forty or fifty. Particularly vulnerable were the officers of the Department of District Administration (previously Native Affairs), whose work experience was hardly relevant to Australian conditions.

By August 1971 we had Sere Pitoi as Chairman of the Public Service Board and Paulias Matane as Head of the Department of Business Development. These were substantive. Four other indigenous officers were acting Heads in the absence of the substantive Heads, on leave or other duties. They were Aisea Taviai, Vincent Eri, John Natera and Sam Piniau, but the middle ranks of the Public Service were still almost entirely white.

As late as September 1972 Ninkama Bomai, the member for Gumine in the Chimbu District, introduced a motion in the House of Assembly:

> That this House calls upon the Government to send a message to the Australian Government: (a) expressing concern at the lengthy delay in presenting a satisfactory and workable scheme for the retention of overseas officers who can offer valuable skills to this country; (b) calling for immediate action to be taken to remove the widespread uncertainty among those officers about their future; and (c) requesting that the officers concerned be kept fully informed of all moves that are made which concerns them.[20]

Debate on the motion was forestalled by the Minister for External Territories persuading an Adelaide businessman, A.M. Simpson, to try once more to put together a scheme acceptable to all parties. This time, his proposals were generally accepted both in Papua New Guinea and in Australia. Some meteoric elevations in the Public Service followed for some indigenous officers — perhaps too meteoric in some cases. Had we been able to resolve the redundancy problem two years earlier, we would have had a much stronger base for the indigenization of the service.

On the Administrative front, things were moving along pretty well. Our "gearing up" programme was to arrange for the transfer of powers and responsibilities and the absorption of functions then carried out by a number of Commonwealth Departments. The submission for the consideration of the AEC listed fifteen of them. In part the submission read:

> (a) Every Commonwealth activity in the Territory so far as it is a function of internal self-government should be regarded as appropriate for transfer. (b) In view of Government policy that Papua New Guinea can have self-government whenever the people say they want it, the transfer to the Administration of the activities concerned should take place as soon as practicable so that the Territory, upon choosing self-government, may be in a position to assume responsibility for all the functions normally associated with internal self-government.[21]

Of the fifteen departmental or agency functions listed for transfer, the major ones were the Commonwealth Department of Works, the Australian Broadcasting Commission and the Department of Civil Aviation, while the last named was linked with the fate of air services to, from and within Papua New Guinea then provided by TAA and Ansett. The 1970–71 Papua New Guinea expenditures for the three major functions just listed were Civil Aviation $7.3 million, Works

$836,000 and ABC $792,000. The airlines, of course, were profit-making concerns, particularly so from the lucrative Sydney/Moresby/Sydney flights. Another highly profitable agency was Overseas Telecommunications. The Commonwealth Department of National Development was also a big spender in Papua New Guinea, using $3.2 million in 1970–71, mostly for oil search subsidies.

As far as Papua New Guinea was concerned the contentious issues were related to the ABC and the airlines. Papua New Guinean Ministers were never greatly concerned about who controlled the back-up services, provided that particular agency footed the bill. The Department of Civil Aviation control of major aerodromes and its policing of rules and regulations was never a sensitive issue, but what happened to the air services which everyone used, and who got the profit, certainly were. Just as important to Papua New Guineans was the control of information outlets, and in a country with a very low literacy level that meant the radio stations. The ABC began broadcasting from Port Moresby in 1946 and it was not until 1961 that the Administration established its first station, in Rabaul, specificially to broadcast to the restless Tolai. The Administration network then expanded and by the end of 1971 there were ten stations, each broadcasting to essentially local audiences with extensive use of the vernacular languages of the individual districts. The ABC catered in general for a broader audience using mostly English, but increasingly some Pidgin and Motu. From time to time commercial interests had expressed interest in obtaining a broadcasting licence for Papua New Guinea but had been rebuffed.

Chatterton set the ball rolling by moving in the House of Assembly on 4 September 1970:

That this House calls on the Administration and the Australian Government to establish without delay a Papua and New Guinea National Broadcasting Commission to take over and extend the broadcasting facilities now operated by the Australian Broadcasting Commission and the Administration, to promote the Territory-wide dissemination of entertainment and information and to provide a forum for the expression of a variety of views on the social, economic and political problems of Papua New Guinea.[22]

The ABC was not too reluctant to surrender its Papua New Guinea responsibilities so that in due course, but not until 1973, Papua New Guinea controlled all broadcasting within the country.

The airlines were tougher to crack. Our belief was that the two-airline system should be replaced by one

The inauguration of the Papua New Guinea National Broadcasting Commission. From left: Sam Piniau, Chairman; Malcolm Naylor, A.B.C. Manager; Kubulan Los, Member; Les Johnson.

Papua New Guinea-owned airline which would take over internal services and share the Australia-Papua New Guinea runs with a nominated Australian carrier, presumably Qantas. It was September 1972 before an agreement was reached. The Director-General of the Department of Civil Aviation, Donald Anderson and I met on Sunday 3 September and put together a package proposal whereby an airline would be set up with TAA, Ansett and Qantas participating with a Papua New Guinea nominee. At the time, the two responsible Ministers, Andrew Peacock for External Territories and Bob Cotton for Civil Aviation, were in Port Moresby, and were persuaded to agree. The AEC fell in line and so Air Niugini was born. There was a deal of argument later about the proportion of shares held by the various parties, and I recall a meeting in Sydney, between Charles Jones, who was Labor's ministerial successor to Cotton, and Michael Somare. Jones rejected Somare's arguments to increase Ansett's ownership share by telling Somare that he could argue till he was black in the face without budging Jones from his position.

The Administration had already given some consideration to foreign affairs and defence, and had begun a training scheme for future foreign service officers, but further action depended on a clearer indication of when Papua New Guinea would require to undertake its own foreign relations. There was no great pressure to do so. The principal debate on defence matters concerned the use of the Pacific Islands Regiment, particularly Administration efforts to persuade the Australian Government to permit the use of troops to assist police to man the border with West Irian. There, police faced a flow of illegal immigrants and a small dissident group were harassing Indonesian installations and using our side of the border as a refuge. The Australian Government was alarmed that the possibility of hot pursuit of a dissident

band might spark an incident and wanted elements of
the Australian Defence Force well out of the way if
such a conflict occurred. In fact there was one such
occasion when some shots were fired on our side of the
border, but it was a minor incident with no repercussions. Anyway we were firmly denied the use of
troops, and some of our restive politicians were beginning to question whether there was any advantage in taking over this expensive but apparently unusable force,
unless Papua New Guinea suffered invasion, or the
threat of it, by a foreign power, in which case they confidently expected that Australia would provide protection. In defence of the Pacific Islands Regiment (PIR), it
should be said that they did perform many useful civil
functions; they assisted us in coping with natural
disasters and in search and rescue operations, and they
operated a village improvement programme, but they
could not be used in any situation which, by Australian
standards, was a police function.

At this time, the Papua New Guinea police resources
were very seriously stretched. A large force was maintained in the Gazelle Peninsula and we also had considerable numbers in Bougainville. At the same time increasing unrest and tribal affrays in the highlands
required that riot squads be held in reserve. Urban
crime was increasing. We needed all the help we could
get. There were also evidences of social strain in
undeveloped areas and the most notable example of this
was a cargo cult movement in the Sepik District led by
one Matthias Yaliwan.[23] Yaliwan preached that the
removal of a cement survey marker from a hilltop
called Mount Turu would release cargo, and all those
who followed him would be rewarded. Admission to
the cult was obtained by the payment of twelve dollars.
There is no doubt that Yaliwan was sincere in his belief,
and he enrolled most of the people from the villages

surrounding his own, some of them on the principle that there might be something in it. As was usual in such cases, work stopped in the gardens which meant a likely food shortage in the area, and the cultists refused to pay local government council taxes.

Yaliwan fixed 7 July 1971 for the removal of the marker and, as there had been some references to sacrifices, we were concerned that there might be a ritual killing, perhaps of Yaliwan himself, or that a riot might follow when the promised cargo did not materialize. We had vividly in mind events in the Madang District some years earlier when there had been a ritual killing in the presence of a horrified Catholic Archbishop. However, we thought it best to stand aside rather than deny the cultists passage to the hilltop. The great day came and a crowd estimated at between six thousand and nine thousand trekked up the hill behind Yaliwan. The marker was removed, no cargo appeared and down they came again to lay the marker at the door of the sub-district office.

Yaliwan's influence waned but it remained sufficient for him to win handsomely a seat in the House of Assembly elections in the following year. His lieutenants then took charge of the movement and converted it into a businesslike money-making operation, at least for the leaders, named the Peli Association. Adherents were directed to purchase a small suitcase and then pass it into a "powerhouse" where young women called "flower girls" were busy making money, it seemed by pouring silver coins from one tin dish into another so that the accompanying noise could be heard by eager cultists outside. The little cases inside the powerhouse were sealed and passed out to the owners who were told to bury them in specially prepared plots made available for ten dollars. On a particular day the cases were to be disinterred in the hope that they would contain large sums of money. Such optimism was usually disappointed but the fortunate few who won the lottery were expected to make a donation to the cult leadership.

With each successive disappointment, followers diminished, but the leaders then produced new rituals and new promises until the faith of the followers was exhausted and the cult died. But Yaliwan took his seat in the House of Assembly and on the first day of the first meeting of the new House he caught the eye of the Speaker and proclaimed his leadership:

> My name is Matthias Yaliwan and I am the elected member for Yangoru-Saussia. It is my wish that I am the leader of Papua New Guinea. It is also my wish that immediate self-government should be achieved followed by immediate independence. That is what I Matthias Yaliwan want.[24]

He was bemused that his claim was completely ignored by his fellow members. His colleague from an adjoining electorate, Pita Lus, attacked him from his cult activities:

> At this point I challenge Mr Yaliwan to let us see the money-making factory, the Yaliwan mint that he is telling his followers about. Let everyone see this factory which is supposed to make a lot of money. . . . When you go back to your electorate I would like you to open this money-making house, to prove to your supporters that it is a reality.[25]

Yaliwan responded that "What the people are doing is what they like doing. I myself have not seen the money. It is the affair of the people. . . . I resigned from the movement because I discovered that its beliefs are not true and I have had nothing whatsoever to do with it since."[26] Yaliwan failed utterly to cope with his parliamentary surroundings and soon ceased attending so that in due course his seat was declared vacant.

At the end of 1971 I summarized the year past in a despatch to the Minister, leading with the tensions caused by social change:

The salient feature of the year has been the nature and extent of social change. Social change is the product of many factors; the introduction of a cash economy and the consequent expansion of horizons; national politics; roads and the changed nature of contacts those roads bring; education; radio; improved health; these are but a few of those factors. They have made a dramatic impact on the minds and lives of the people. Even when the outward manifestations of change are hardly apparent, men and women are trying to cope with new concepts and rearranging their thoughts and their lives accordingly. Often this leads to uncertainty and confusion, to the breakdown of social controls before the new kind of society has its own established mores. It leads to a search for explanations which often results in bizarre beliefs and practices.

Arising from this situation there has been a growing disregard for the established law and for those administering it, which has resulted in a substantial increase of violent crime. The excessive social strains seem likely to continue for this decade and beyond.

Another of the obvious results of social change has been the changed nature of race relations; some would call it a deterioration, but I think that this would be a misinterpretation of what is happening. The master/servant relationship — or, in the more enlightened section of the community, that of tutor/student — is no longer tenable as a means of social differentiation. Those who persist in regarding Papuans and New Guineans in this light provoke anger, resentment and rejection. In general, race relationships remain amicable, but there are tensions which occasionally result in expressions or demonstrations of antipathy. Papuans and New Guineans do not resent expatriates with high levels of skills, nor is there much criticism of the pay they get, but increasingly there is criticism and jealousy of unskilled and semi-skilled young expatriates enjoying a standard of living far above that of their

Papuan and New Guinean colleagues. The repatriation of this class of European is unlikely to proceed fast enough to avoid numbers of unpleasant incidents in the next year or two. In particular this will remain a constant source of irritation to the young educated Papuans and New Guineans.

The more apparent expressions of the tensions referred to above have been the subject of earlier surveys: the continuing intransigence of the Mataungan Association, the various cargo-cult movements, most notably the Yaliwan-led cult in the Sepik; the incidents of violence in the Highlands; and the proliferation of movements which are in part a search for identity and in part designed to tap the material riches of modern society: Napidakoe Navitu, Nemea, Damuni, Tutu-kuvul Kapkapis Association (TKA) and the Mataungan Association are examples. The growth of understanding and the development of more logical patterns of thought may transmute all of these into movements working through normal political and economic channels to attain legitimate ends. (Napidakoe has already gone this way.) Most of the groups mentioned appear to be moving in this direction in that they are nominating candidates for the 1972 elections, though it must be understood that participation in a national election does not necessarily mean the acceptance of the other trappings of government. At least for the time being most of these movements will preach a disregard for the law — or some of it — and maintain anti-government stances.[27]

In some respects it had been a pretty rough year, in others a very satisfying one. I looked forward to 1972 with some optimism.

NOTES

1. Address by E.G. Whitlam, Monash University, 29 July 1971, PP.
2. The Southern Highlands was the only highlands district within Papua.
3. P.N.G., House of Assembly Debates (HAD), vol. II, no. 13, p. 3818.
4. Press conference, 12 August 1971, PP.

5. Statement by L.W. Johnson, 20 May 1971, quoted in P.N.G., HAD, vol. II, no. 14, p. 4158.
6. P.N.G., HAD, vol. II, no. 14, p. 4157.
7. Ibid., p. 4174.
8. Ibid., p. 4261.
9. The Ministers were Oala Rarua, Lokoloko, Kapena, Watson and Wabiria. Guise, the Speaker, after kicking up a fuss, was included.
10. P.N.G., HAD, vol. II, no. 19, p. 5129.
11. Administrator to Minister, 28 December 1971, PP.
12. Speech, 6 July 1967, reprinted in *Planning for Tomorrow*, Commonwealth Government Printer, Canberra.
13. P.N.G., HAD, vol. II, no. 14, p. 4320.
14. Any occupation, the products from which are sold for money.
15. Speech delivered 18 October 1971, script among PP.
16. Johnson to Hay, 25 January 1971, PP.
17. The other was that of Deputy Administrator.
18. McKinnon to Administrator, 23 November 1970, PP.
19. Notes of discussion on accelerated promotion, 17 July 1971, PP.
20. P.N.G., HAD, vol. II, no. 8, p. 971.
21. AEC submission, June 1971, PP.
22. P.N.G., HAD, vol. II, no. 11, p. 3123.
23. Sometimes rendered as "Yeliwan".
24. P.N.G., HAD, vol. III, no. 1, p. 13.
25. P.N.G., HAD, vol. III, no. 2, p. 220.
26. Ibid., p. 221.
27. Administrator to Minister, 28 December 1971, PP.

6

THE NEW MEN

On 26 January 1972 C.E. Barnes left the Ministry and was replaced by Andrew Peacock, then in his early thirties and previously Minister for the Army. This has been considered by some as the beginning of a new era, but it was hardly so. The initiative had come from Prime Minister Gorton in July 1970. By the end of that year the transfer of power to the Ministers of Papua New Guinea had been effected, even if they had made but modest use of it. Early in 1971, the Papua New Guinea Select Committee on Constitutional Development had made its report, which had been accepted by the House of Assembly and by the Australian Government. We had the parameters of a target date for self-government and had put together a team to set about planning the progressive transfer of the whole range of activities still carried out by Australian Government instrumentalities. What we awaited was the result of the next elections for the third House of Assembly, due in February 1972, to give us a further indication of the pace at which we would be required to travel. If the conservatives, gathered together in the United Party, had a firm majority, self-government might be delayed until 1975 or 1976. If the progressives, with the Pangu

Party in the van, won the day 1973 or 1974 was more likely.

Barnes, over a period of eight years, had presided over remarkable social, economic and political changes in Papua New Guinea. The office he had undertaken was hardly suited to his interests or his experience, and he was out of tune with what might be termed the progressive elements in Papua New Guinea society, but he was steadfast and loyal to his subordinates and all of those who worked for him held him in warm regard, even when disagreeing with his conservative approach to political development. I think that we would all agree that he was a true gentleman in the broadest sense of the word.

What Peacock brought to Papua New Guinea was a new approach rather than new policies. He was young enough to relate to the youthful Papua New Guinean politicians, he was forthcoming, eminently approachable and eager. He had political style and was in tune with the changes initiated by his Prime Minister. Instead of the reluctant political concessions of the Barnes–Warwick Smith era, there was a welcome to those Papua New Guineans keen to take over responsibility for their own country. Peacock was Minister for External Territories for less than a year but he did put his stamp on the political changes in the climactic year of 1972.

The last meeting of the second House of Assembly was in November 1971, but it set the scene for the 1972 elections. Combat between the contending parties was joined on the first day of the meeting, when there was an angry debate between the supporters of the United and Pangu parties concerning political pamphlets purportedly emanating from political party sources. There were some very unparliamentary exchanges between Michael Somare and Tei Abal, the leaders of the contending parties. Of course a deal of misinformation was circulating, sponsored by protagonists of the major parties, who exercised their own discretion as to the content of political pamphlets. It was a crucial election, the first real contest for political power, and for the perquisites that go with it. Individual members were only too conscious of their vulnerability, given their inability to satisfy even a small proportion of the demands of their electors. One device proposed to safeguard their position was to double the nomination deposit for candidates from fifty dollars to one hundred dollars. Pangu Pati members, supported by independents such as Percy Chatterton and Father Nilles, objected: "What are we doing here? We are saying 'Right, we are the Members of the House. We can afford to put up a deposit of one hundred dollars so we can stop the ordinary villagers who want to contest a seat. . . .' Thus we are interfering with human rights and the freedom of choice."[1] But the might of highland voters was too much and the Bill to increase the deposit passed, though contested hotly all the way down to the wire. The final division saw 45 supporting votes with only 12 opposed. There were many abstentions where conscience and self-interest were in conflict.

The quarrel about political pamphleteering continued throughout the meeting. Both parties produced evidence of unethical practices. The United Party was pilloried for circulating a letter among highland students[2] putting forward arguments to delay self-government and independence by supporting United Party candidates: "There are quite a few smart coastal fellows who . . . have realized that now is their time to get all the top positions in the Government and in private enterprise. They have put us in the grass-cutting level and reckon that we will always be there. . . . Just because of our late discovery and late start in education our fellows who have some education are only junior officers."[3]

However, the House concluded without any blows being struck on 23 November 1971 and on the invitation of the Speaker I had some soothing words to say:

> If we are all here today, we have twenty-three of those who were present when the first House of Assembly meeting began in 1964, 21 elected members, Mr Newman and I. I think that we were all proud to be here on that important occasion and very naturally we are proud to be here still. But in 1964 we were uncertain about our role and indeed, of our future. Now this uncertainty has gone. The House knows its present powers and influence and uses them. The House knows that the third House of Assembly elected next year is likely to be the most important one in the past and future history of Papua New Guinea. That House may well have to choose the constitutional path on which we finally travel.[4]

I used a little Pidgin to conclude.

> Taim mi lukluk raun long haus, mi hamamas long lukim planti pren bilong olgeta hap bilong Papua New Guinea. I gat sampela New Guineans sampela Papuans, sampela Australians, na sampela bilong ol arapela kantri tu, tasol, yumi olgeta ibin wok wantaim long girapim Papua New Guinea. Namba tu Haus of Asembli ibin bringim Papua New Guinea pinis long doa bilong taim emi kamap olsem wanpela kantri ai ting bai namba tri Haus inap long opim dispela doa bai yumi ken go insait long dispela taim.[5]

That night my wife and I gave a wind-up party for them all, including officials and the press corps. The Speaker was kind enough to expand my guest list somewhat: "Those who are married may take their wives with them. For those who have no wives, I suggest that they take one girl friend only, not two."[6] I'm not sure how many restrained themselves to that counsel, for about three hundred turned up and consumed alarming amounts of food and drink.

The second House of Assembly was over. It had been dominated throughout by the conservatives, with the numbers coming from the large Highlands bloc supported both financially and organizationally by white private interests, sometimes aided and abetted by individual public servants; but it had seen the progressive interests get a firm foothold in Parliament and there had been a strong growth in the influence of indigenous public servants outside parliament. As for the Government, epitomized in Papua New Guinea by the Administrator and his senior officers, it seemed that we would continue to have a strong influence on policy in the event of a conservative majority being returned to the third House of Assembly. If progressive elements managed to muster the numbers, we would be looking at a significantly earlier date for self-government and the need for an accelerated programme for the devolution of powers and the transfer of responsibilities.

For the new Minister, Andrew Peacock, David Hay provided a general assessment nominating the critical problems as follows:

   (I) Definition of Australia's national interest against the time when P.N.G. becomes independent. At present the UN Charter sets out our obligations. These will, formally, be discharged at independence.

  (II) National unity. The Government has not taken a formal stand on what it would do if, e.g., Bougainville sought to secede.

 (III) Planning of and preparation for the handover of the remaining powers.

 (IV) The timetable of movement to internal self-government.

  (V) The Judiciary and court systems.

 (VI) The strengthening of the police force, and the role of the Army in internal security.

(VII) Citizenship. There is no Papua New Guinea citizenship. Expatriates, who may have no long term intention of staying in Papua New Guinea, are able to exercise considerable political and economic influence.

(VIII) The structure of government in P.N.G. — in particular, the distribution of power between the centre and the districts.

(XI) Commonwealth aid policy.

(X) The setting of goals for national development and the preparation of a national development programme to be put into effect when the present five year programme ends in 1973.

(XI) The social problems consequent upon economic development, e.g. urban drift, school dropouts.

(XII) The preservation of P.N.G.'s cultural and natural heritage.

(XIII) Relations with Japan and other foreign investors. Australia's future role in investments.[7]

Hay continued by outlining some of the uncertainties so that the new Minister would be left with no illusions about his new portfolio. These included the lack of accepted leaders prepared to accept responsibility, the dependence on expatriates to sustain the administrative framework, the dominance of the economy by expatriate interests, the crucial role of the Australian grant and likely Australian pressures to change its nature, and the problems arising from the likely divergence of interests between Australia and Papua New Guinea. He concluded:

In these circumstances much is going to depend on the quality of decisions taken by the Commonwealth over the next few months and years. But perhaps more will depend on the establishment of relations of mutual confidence between the Commonwealth and New Guinea Governments. In this your own role will be critically important. If you succeed, then Papua New Guinea leaders will look to you and consult you on all important decisions. They will ring you up or ask to see you frequently. This will do much to ensure a smooth transition and a friendly relationship thereafter. It is hardly necessary to emphasize the importance for building up a relationship of confidence and of your knowing the country and its people as intimately as possible.[8]

The Minister took this advice to heart and paid his first visit to Papua New Guinea immediately after perusing the memo, arriving on 3 February. He wasted no time in accepting speaking engagements, the first occasion being on 15 February 1972 at the first meeting of the Board of the Investment Corporation, when he referred to its role as promoting partnership between local and overseas investors, thus enabling Papua New Guineans to benefit from the development of major projects and "to achieve a firm grip on their country's economic management".[9] At the University graduation ceremony in Port Moresby on 3 March he referred to self-government. "The Government believes it should help Papua New Guinea move towards self-government; it should not just sit back and wait for it to happen. . . . We encourage the desire for self-government in Papua New Guinea but we are waiting for the people to tell us when they want it."[10]

It was a theme to be repeated in an address to a Liberal Party meeting in Brisbane. "We believe we should encourage the desire for self-government but we are waiting for the House of Assembly to speak itself or to indicate some way in which the wishes of the people of Papua New Guinea on this question can be clearly seen."[11] The key words which later required careful definition were "some way in which the wishes of the people can be clearly seen".

Meanwhile the political parties, the small non-aligned groups and the ambitious individuals were around and about distributing pamphlets exhorting electors,

Investiture at Government House, Papua New Guinea, 1972. From left: Michael Somare, Dulcie Johnson, Andrew Peacock.

spreading kindness, information and misinformation; and also spreading a little cash and other tangible rewards around to the faithful or to those who, it was hoped, would prove to be faithful at the ballot box.

I have referred earlier to the two major parties, the United Party and the Pangu Pati, and to their leaders. Tei Abal, Chairman of the United Party, was a self-taught highlander from Wabag in the Western Highlands, now the Enga Province. He had served in both the first and second Houses of Assembly. He had been a Minister and a member of the Executive Council. He had never been to school and spoke no English, but was literate in Pidgin. Tei epitomized the highlanders' strong conservatism, in so far as early self-government was concerned. In 1972 he was forty years of age. Michael Somare was thirty-five years old and had entered parliament in 1968, representing his home district, East Sepik. Prior to that he had been a teacher, then a journalist. By Papua New Guinea standards he was well educated, having had the equivalent of three years of secondary education plus teacher training courses and later specialized training at the Administrative College. He was the exact antithesis of Tei Abal. He wanted immediate self-government, he was critical of the Administration and all its works, though experience in the second House of Assembly had matured him. He had an attractive, open personality and I had always found him reasonable and responsible.

The People's Progress Party, generally known as the PPP, had emerged late in the life of the second House of Assembly, having been transformed from a discussion group among like-minded members. Its leader, Julius Chan, was part Chinese, part New Guinean, and like the majority of residents of similar racial origins in Papua New Guinea, was an Australian citizen who had been educated in Australia. He had gathered together a small group of better educated members, those who were moderate conservatives but reluctant to be identified with the United Party. He had originally been an Administration officer but in 1972 was in private business. He was thirty-two, rather a low key man but thoughtful and intelligent.

There were a number of otherf groups and we could anticipate a strong electoral showing from the Mataungan candidates in East New Britain and from the secessionists in Bougainville. There were four seats the Mataungans could possibly win and four to be contested in Bougainville. In the Highlands District — Eastern, Western, Southern and Chimbu — there were 36 seats; in a House of 100 voting members the key to power lay in the unity of the highland members. However, that unity had dissipated with the advent of Thomas Kavali, who won a by-election for the seat of Jimi in the Western Highlands in 1969. He was twenty-seven years old and had previously been a prison warder. He soon distanced himself from his highland colleagues and was more at home with the Pangu Pati members. It was a breach in the Highlands Districts unity and with the approach of the elections Kavali went further and set up a separate highlands party, the New Guinea National Party, which in effect was a projection of Pangu Pati policies in the highlands. If this party made inroads into the United Party's dominance of the highlands the nature of Papua New Guinean politics could change significantly. Kavali certainly intended that it should do so.

Speaking in the last meeting of the second House he castigated the United Party — "the United Party is damaging the morale of the people who are capable of running our country. This United Party is a perfidious party. It should be abolished. The United Party has no planned policy!"[12] He was speaking in Pidgin. I wish I could recall how "perfidious" came out in that language.

The 1972 election was the first one in which the photograph of each candidate appeared on the ballot paper. This was designed to assist illiterate voters and to minimize the use of "whisper vote" whereby an illiterate would whisper his choice to an electoral officer who would record it for him. In three elections we had found no abuse of the whisper vote or malfeasance by electoral officers, but this time we had to be particularly careful, because we had invited a United Nations delegation to observe the elections. The mission was led by W. Tapley Bennett from the U.S.A. and its other members were from Afghanistan, Yugoslavia and the U.K. They were present in Papua New Guinea throughout the voting which began on 19 February and concluded on 11 March.

The best objective account of the election was produced by the United Nations group in Supplement no. 2 to the official records of the 39th Session of the Trusteeship Council. The mission commented that "the dominant issue in these elections, was self-government, not so much whether, but when, it should come. All parties and most independent candidates, took a position on this ranging from 'self-government now' to 'not until we are ready' ".[13] The mission also gave us a good conduct badge: "The Mission began and would like to end this chapter of its report by commending the thoroughness and fairness with which the 1972 Papua New Guinea elections were conducted."[14]

In all, 553 candidates stood for the eighty-two open electorates and 58 for the eighteen regional electorates.[15] Four women stood as candidates. Two candidates were elected unopposed, Michael Somare for the East Sepik regional seat and Brere Awol for West Sepik Coastal. One candidate died during the course of the election, so those nominations had to be recalled and voting deferred until later. Thus the election filled ninety-nine seats, four officials were to be nominated and the House could, if it wished, nominate three additional members, an option which was never taken up.

To meet the expectation of the politically sophisticated, each of the parties produced a platform, though the use of the word "platform" confused some of the less erudite electors, as had the word "party" earlier. The United Party produced a document so bland that anyone could subscribe to it. Among other things it aimed "to raise the living standards of the people", "to develop an educational system that would enable the people of Papua New Guinea to participate fully in all affairs of the country". It had eventually become convinced of the virtues of a party system for now it "regards the development of a strong party system as essential". It no longer flinched at the words "self-government" and "independence" though there were undertones of caution in its statements; for instance, it aimed "to develop a strong economic system by which an independent Papua New Guinea could support such a system of government", while it considered that "a pre-requisite for independence is the development of experienced political leaders at the council, area, regional and national levels" and it further believed that "the final decision for independence and the date for independence should be taken up by the House of Assembly after it has ascertained the desires of the people of the country." The United Party was confident that it had the voters in the highlands sewn up — its platform was aimed more at persuading votes from the middle ground.

The Peoples' Progress Party also aimed to be all things to almost all men but it was precise about its commitment to private enterprise. It aimed "to recognize, encourage and protect private enterprise through individual participation". It also wished "to preserve democracy through the parliamentary system of government and the rule of law" and it proclaimed its intention "to build a nation dedicated to political and religious liberty and freedom and dignity of man". The party sat on the fence on the timing of self-government. Its concern was that "Papua New Guinea should get the type of government its people deserve; strong, stable, progressive government."

The Pangu Pati was more specific. It nailed its colours firmly to the mast on self-government. It declared for "self-government now" and stressed that, to prepare for it, it was necessary to have better political education, quicker localization of senior public service posts and in business and to have strong political parties. It was also going to solve land problems by, once more, putting an expert committee to work, and it aimed to provide at least eight years of education for all children. It also undertook to help Workers' unions to obtain better pay and conditions.[16]

The major parties seemed to have a deal of money to spend on electioneering, but they were all shy about acknowledging the sources of it. Japanese interests, with an eye to the future, made contributions, while Australian businessmen in Papua New Guinea and the plantation community were firmly behind the United Party. Much of the limited PPP campaign was self-financed or dependent on contributions from business associates, relatives and friends.

Although there appeared to be a lot of interest in the election there was rather a disappointing turnout to vote, although voting was not compulsory. We had hoped for a voting figure of seventy to eighty per cent of the eligible population but achieved only about sixty per cent, due, in part, to the extreme difficulty of getting officials and ballot boxes to every hamlet, and perhaps also to the apathy of short term expatriates in the towns who thought it was none of their business anyway. Disillusionment among villagers, because, in eight years of House of Assembly promises, not too much cargo had been delivered, also limited their eagerness to exercise their democratic rights.

Prior to the election I had estimated that the state of the House might turn out to be about forty UP members, twenty–twenty-five Pangu and ten PPP, with the remainder non-aligned. But the move away from the UP was stronger than I had forecast. Of those who acknowledged a party loyalty prior to the election, twenty-eight UP members were elected, nineteen Pangu, and seven PPP. There were three Mataungans and Kavali was the only acknowledged member of his own National Party. That left forty-one with no openly asserted affiliation. It was a pack full of wild cards.

Of the 74 elected members of the second House of Assembly who contested the election, 38 were returned, a proportion of success similar to that in the two previous elections, but there were certainly some surprises among the defeated. Tom Leahy, the Spokesman for the AEC, was the tallest poppy to go, defeated on his own patch by an obscure New Guinean who was a domestic servant in Lae, but also a member of the Pangu Pati. Leahy contributed to his own downfall by failing to resist an invitation to join the Australian delegation to the UN Trusteeship Council meeting in New York, as an adviser, when he might have been campaigning for re-election. The Pangu executive had specifically set out to topple Leahy, and after the event wrote to him to tell him why:—

> Within the United Party there are Tom Leahy, Dennis Buchanan and Bill Fielding in general agreement. We feel that Tom Leahy is the basic force behind this con-

sensus. None of these others [the European members of the UP] by themselves or in any other combination can hold the United Party together as it is today. . . . Tom Leahy is the force behind Tei Abal and Tom Leahy and Dennis Buchanan are the force behind Sinake Giregire.

These two are the main contenders for the leadership of the United Party and hence Prime Ministership if the United Party is able and willing to accept government. . . . Our reluctant conclusion was this. If we remove Tom Leahy, the United Party will not be in a position to put up or at least to maintain a Prime Minister.[17]

Labyrinthine stuff, but anyway Leahy lost, as did the other two Australians referred to, Buchanan and Fielding. In fact most of the leading expatriate figures in the United Party disappeared, leaving only three of the originals — Ron Neville, John Middleton and Tim Ward. Nine expatriates were elected as against twenty in the previous smaller House. Tony Voutas, one of the creators of the Pangu Pati, did not stand, preferring that the leadership of the party should be clearly seen as Papua New Guinean. As mentioned previously, Josephine Abaijah, the personable Papuan separatist, was successful. Ten members had served in both previous Houses. Of these, Guise, Toliman, Abal, Lapun, Giregire, Lus and Neville had all figured prominently in the country's affairs. Those re-elected for a second term included Somare, Chan, Arek (who had chaired the second Constitutional Select Committee), Tammur, the Patron of the Mataungan Association, Lokoloko, the Deputy Spokesman of the AEC, and Kavali, the cuckoo in the highland's nest. Of the newcomers some were already prominent figures on the Papua New Guinea landscape — John Momis, a Catholic Priest, a prominent Bougainville secessionist, John Kaputin, a Mataungan spokesman and Albert Maori Kiki, a leading figure in the Pangu Pati. The Pangu parliamentary representatives were quite an impressive bunch, mostly youthful, mostly pretty well educated by P.N.G. standards and with a solid core of parliamentary experience. The UP still had its principal indigenous leadership but its numerical strength was based in highlands members, most of whom had little or no education. The practice of the highlands electors of trying out a new member in each election meant that they were short of parliamentary experience.

The election results certainly left the issue as to which party would get the numbers to form a government wide open.

NOTES

1. P.N.G., House of Assembly Debates (HAD), vol. II, no. 19, p. 5113.
2. Voting age had dropped, and eighteen-year-olds were eligible to vote.
3. P.N.G., HAD, vol. II, no. 20, p. 5309.
4. Administrator's address to House of Assembly, 23 November 1971, PP.
5. Translation: "As I look around the House I am proud to say that I can see many friends from all parts of Papua New Guinea. There are New Guineans and Papuans and Australians and some from other countries too, but we have all worked together for the good of Papua New Guinea. The second House of Assembly has brought Papua New Guinea to the door of nationhood, the third House may well open that door so that we may enter."
6. P.N.G., HAD, vol. II, no. 20, p. 5284.
7. Memo Hay to Peacock, 1 February 1972, PP.
8. Ibid.
9. Selected Ministerial Statements on Papua New Guinea, February — July 1972, AGPS, Canberra, p. 7.
10. Ibid., 3 March 1972, p. 9.
11. Ibid., 8 april 1972, p. 12.
12. P.N.G., HAD, vol. II, no. 20, p. 5313.
13. Page 37 of the report.
14. Page 38 of the report.
15. Regional candidates were required to have at least three years of secondary education or its equivalent. Equivalence was generously interpreted.

16. All election campaign quotations from the House of Assembly Elections 1972, Department of Information and Extension Services, January 1972.
17. Christine Voutas to Tom Leahy, 6 February 1972 but delivered on 23 March 1972, PP.

7

A NATIONAL COALITION

The counting of votes began on 11 March and, although it was a protracted process, by 26 March most of the results were complete and there was plenty of time for political alliances to occur before the House was to meet for the first time on 20 April 1972. As indicated previously there were forty-one members who, on the face of it, were open for wooing. At this time I thought that a coalition of the United Party with conservative independents and the PPP was most likely to provide a parliamentary majority, but the UP was curiously inactive at first in seeking adherents. This was in part due to the loss of the leadership of the four defeated expatriates, Leahy, Lussick, Fielding and Buchanan, and in part to the over-optimistic expectation that they would have the numbers anyway.

The constitutional position was such that I, wearing my Head of State hat, could not call upon one group or the other to form a government, as the numbers were too indefinite. Which party had a definite majority would have to be proved on the floor of the House and the first crucial vote would be on the membership of the Ministerial Nominations Committee, the committee elected by the House to consult with the Administrator

on a ministerial list which then had to go back to the
House for ratification. It was the division in the House
on membership of this Committee that would point up
the majority party or the majority coalition. A publication on Papua New Guinea has asserted that I was
directed in writing by the Minister for External Territories not to accept an exclusively United Party team
of Ministers from the Committee.[1] This is quite in-
correct. I was given no such directive. We would have
lived with whatever team the House produced, though
we would have worked hard to ensure that the list did
not include more than one or two expatriates.

The Pangu Pati leadership was on the job early.
Somare, Kiki and Voutas called on me on 20 March,
followed on the next day by Leahy, still shattered by his
defeat. Guise followed close on their heels to explain to
me his design to gather a third force together which
could be the balance between two factions, and
presumably project him into the top political post. Then
Toliman and Abal, the indigenous leaders of the UP and
John Middleton, a prosperous Australian planter from
the island of Kar Kar off Madang and likely to be the
leading expatriate in the UP, called in. Chan stayed in
his tent (but not sulking) in Rabaul waiting for offers!

I said the same thing to all my visitors. Here follow
my notes dictated at the time:

> It appeared unlikely that any one party could achieve a
> majority on its own and that a party could only form a
> government by association with other individuals and
> groups. If either the United Party or the Pangu Pati was
> excluded from the Government, their numbers in the
> House would be sufficient to make firm and consistent
> government very difficult. . . .
>
> If a United Party Government was formed with the
> aid of PPP and sympathetic independents, the most
> possible eventuality, a Ministry chosen from their ranks
> would be a very limited one and would have to include

a good many Ministers with little or no education, some entirely illiterate. It was hard to envisage effective government in these circumstances and Ministers would be under serious handicaps in advancing and defending their policies in the House.

A Government based on the Pangu Pati would also suffer from its domination by the youthful elite group and the highlands bloc would be isolated and alienated. This would pose dangerous problems for any Government. . . .

One possibility would be a Government comprising elements of the two major parties by evolving some mutually acceptable formula. Messrs Voutas and Somare indicated agreement as far as they personally were concerned but said that they would have difficulty in being part of a Ministry which might include Giregire and be influenced by Neville. They also said that elements within their own party may prevent any kind of association with members of the United Party.

Guise, still with leadership hopes, was intent on gathering what he called a "third force" around him which would align itself with the Pangu Pati and thus become an important part of Government. Guise assured me that he would never become a member of Pangu, though I had quite reliable information that he had, originally at any rate, been a member. I told him that he would need to be assured of about twenty followers if he were to influence events. Even so, a Government without the consent of the forty or so United Party members would be difficult. A Guise following would consist essentially of those independents who would have, in general, supported Pangu policies in any case.[2]

Somare, Guise and Abal or their emissaries had all approached Chan of the PPP, who had seven or eight adherents, but he had made no commitments to anyone. It was possible that if Chan moved into a Pangu coalition, he would split his party anyway and his value to an alliance would be diminished.

As 20 April approached the counting of heads

became a more precise process. It seemed that the UP had forty-four members and if the PPP could be coaxed into a coalition, and with the support of a few like-minded independents, a Centre–Right government could be put together, albeit with an uncertain majority. Party representatives shuttled around the country trying to persuade the uncommitted and it was alleged that the United Party was offering lump sums of money in return for a conversion. The PPP, both elected and defeated members, met in Rabaul and reportedly made a tentative decision to join the UP in a coalition in return for four or five Ministerial posts, but no one party could yet exhibit sufficient support to convince the waverers.

Members began gathering in Port Moresby on the weekend of 15–16 April and lobbying became intensive. Parties set up airport patrols to catch the uncommitted at the threshhold. Early on, a UP/PPP coalition still seemed the most likely eventuality. Having previously seen the leader of UP and Pangu, I asked the PPP leaders to see me and I had a discussion with Chan, Dutton and Boas on 18 April. Chan asked me for my views and I said that I could not see enough support for either UP or Pangu and that in these circumstances the attitude of PPP was crucial. Chan claimed to have ten members — a not unexpected growth in strength when the strong bargaining position of the party was realized. I said that I thought a group that could muster fifty-five votes in the House against forty-four Opposition would have a reasonable chance of forming a stable government. (This might seem more than a comfortable majority but, given the propensity of members to change their minds and the possibility of unpredictable absences, a substantial cushion of adherents was essential for continuity of government.) I further said that the tide of colonial history indicated that a Centre/Right coalition might have defectors to more progressive forces in the course of the first year or so of office and could lose its floor majority. Chan gave no indication of the likely attitude of his party and indeed, it was clear that his party was divided on the partnership issue.

Pangu, with more sophisticated political strategists, had been busy lobbying the younger new members and had made some significant gains, particularly among highland members from the Chimbu. Pangu was so desperate to muster the numbers that Somare, despite strong opposition from Kiki, offered Guise the leadership if he would join them publicly. Guise temporized, as he too doubted that the numbers were there, and lost his chance for leadership. On the evening of 18 April Somare announced firmly that he had fifty-one supporters, — party members and fellow travellers. It was a doubtful claim, but there had been some defectors from the United Party, notably a previous Minister, Kaibelt Diria, who reportedly had missed out on a party honorarium of two hundred dollars and had changed sides on the expectation of continuing in the Ministry in a Pangu government. Kavali's Nationalist Party also claimed ten members following the Pangu flag.

The ranks of the United Party were in a state of some confusion. There was no coherent organization and no central executive capable of planning a strategy and executing it. Potential allies, notably the PPP, saw that they would face an uncertain future allied with the UP and the party met again on 19 April to consider the position. The meeting lasted for five hours with sharp divisions evident. However, ultimately the party decided to ally itself with Pangu. Some PPP members thought of resigning from the party but considered that they would lose all opportunity to exercise a moderating influence on the coalition. They were also not unmindful of the price Pangu paid for their support as Chan had demanded four Ministries — hardly a modest requirement for a party of ten members.

Whatever the reasons, PPP passed into the coalition intact and that night Somare and Chan announced the alliance. Somare stated that he had the support of fifty-nine members made up of thirty-one Pangu, ten Nationalists, ten PPP, three Mataungans and five independents. It became known as the National Coalition Government or NCG.

Parliament opened the following day with two crucial votes to test Somare's claim of majority support. The first test of strength was in the election of a Speaker, Pangu-nominated Perry Kwan of the PPP, of part Chinese origin, as part of the price demanded by the PPP. It must have been a bitter pill for Pangu to

Opening of the third House of Assembly. The Governor-General, Sir Paul Hasluck is seated, top centre, flanked by Andrew Peacock, Minister for External Territories (right), and Perry Kwan, Speaker of the House of Assembly (left).

swallow as they had previously canvassed Arek who told me that he had refused, in the hope of a Ministerial post. The UP put up the popular Toliman.

It was a near thing, Kwan forty-nine, Toliman forty-eight, and one informal vote — an indecipherable one, but possibly from Yaliwan. Kwan told me that he had voted for Toliman — a rather unexpected old-world courtesy and hardly the act of a professional politician. The coalition did not seem to be too firmly in the saddle.

For the second and more important vote, the election of the Ministerial Nominations Committee, the new coalition was better organized. They put up a slate comprised of what might be called the coalition leadership group, and one that was nicely calculated to keep the disparate elements in line and perhaps extract a vote or two from the opposition. It was —

Chairman: Somare — Pangu
Members: Guise — independent
           Chan — PPP
           Kavali — NP
           Diria — NP
           Boas — PPP
           Lapun — Pangu

They had no problems this time, winning fifty-five to forty-two, seven highlanders voting with the coalition. The House then adjourned until Monday, the coalition being reluctant to face the House until it had done some more work to consolidate its majority.

I asked that the leadership group see me on Saturday morning and Somare, Guise, Chan and Kavali came along. It was agreed that our discussions should be private and no press statement would be made. We had a general talk about the fragility of the coalition and the need to be cautious in the early months of its life. I pointed out the constitutional position and the need for the time being to conform to the portfolio arrangements of the previous House with only minor modifications until the current *Papua New Guinea Act* could be amended. I suggested that Police and Defence should be set aside until there had been substantive discussions on constitutional development with the Australian Government. Somare was receptive but Guise non-committal. Chan gave the impression that he regarded his party's role as being a brake on the radical proclivities of the Pangu Pati. There was not much evidence of coalition solidarity. However, it seemed to be agreed that May would be occupied with the business of settling in with no pronounced initiatives, with the purpose of getting through the June meeting of the House with an intact majority. The Minister for External Territories had agreed that a group of Ministers, probably Somare, Guise and Chan, would visit Canberra on 10 and 11 May for budget discussions with the Minister and that longer term planning would be for substantive constitutional discussions with the Australian Government in July. I mentioned that the June meeting of the House the further establishment of a Select Committee on Constitutional Development might be considered.

We also had a brief discussion about the make-up of a ministerial group. Somare and Chan both said that they wanted the best possible Ministry, irrespective of regional considerations. Guise, a good deal longer in the head, thought that regional affiliations were an important consideration. Somare had a considerable problem within his party if he was not to disappoint some and perhaps suffer defections as a result. The fact that three well-educated foundation members — Taureka, Kiki and Rea — were all Central District members was a difficulty. I thought that he might get around it by appointing some as "members assisting the Minister", for although these members could not receive any more pay, there would be status and perquisites associated with the appointment. In the event Somare did not take up the idea. He undertook that the Ministerial Nominations Committee would provide me with a ministerial list on the Monday (24 April) and I promised that, subject to any disagreements I might have, I would get the nominations back to the House on the Wednesday.

The weekend was a trying one for many with ministerial aspirations. The terms of the amended *Papua New Guinea Act* passed in 1971 limited the number of Ministers to seventeen and only ten could be in the inner circle — members of the AEC. The PPP had already claimed four posts and Kavali would expect Ministries for his followers. Of the independents supporting Somare, the most active in seeking a post was Paulus Arek — the Chairman of the second Constitutional Committee. He implored almost everyone whom he thought might influence the decision to recommend him, and leaving nothing to chance, telephoned me to enlist my support.

As undertaken, Somare provided me with his list on Monday morning. There were no particular surprises and, after all, the choices showed due attention to regional politics. I thought it inappropriate to try to influence the choice of Ministers, though I saw my role as advisory, but to maintain my statutory position I commented on the overall structure of the list. I considered that the Highlands Districts were under-represented and Somare, more out of courtesy than conviction, included Sasakila Moses from the Eastern Highlands — a selection which did not add too much to the quality of the Ministry, or to its prestige in the eyes of the public. I also commented on likely difficulties on the proposed allocation of Olewale to Education. He was an ex-teacher of no great professional standing. Taureka, a doctor of modest reputation, as Health Minister also seemed an appointment of doubtful wisdom. For fairly obvious reasons Somare thought they were suitable for the allotted tasks and persisted in his choice. Both were unsuccessful in these portfolios because the senior staff in their departments were unable to offer them loyal support. Later on they changed places, and friction between the two Departments and their Ministers subsided. For the record I append to this chapter one of my letters to Somare on allocation of portfolios.

The PPP held the Ministries of Finance, Transport, Business Development and of Trade and Industry — a strong hand in economic development policy and its execution. Jephcott, a cattle farmer, and the only white member, became Minister for Transport.

The Ministry was a good deal stronger in personal attainments than any of its predecessors. With the exception of Guise they were all relatively young men and most had had a substantial amount of education and a variety of work experience, though seven had not previously been in parliament. Only Diria was totally illiterate — it would not be too much to say that he was the token Minister for the undeveloped Western–Southern Highlands. He was originally allocated to the Ministry of Information, which seemed a curious choice for an illiterate. At my suggestion he was moved over to the technical Ministry of Posts and Telegraphs where the Director, Bill Carter, was only too willing to provide guidance. All Ministers except Diria and Moses understood English though a number did not read or speak it with any facility.

Before the list was presented to the House I convened a meeting of the Ministry for the purpose of electing Somare to head up the new Government — in effect to become Chief Minister. There was no statutory provision for such a title but the *Papua New Guinea Act* provided for a deputy to the Administrator in the AEC. Officially Somare became Deputy Chairman of the Administrator's Executive Council — a clumsy title which was never used. Somare was usually known as "The Chief" by those around him and referred to more formally as "Chief Minister".

The inner ring of the Ministry were those members appointed to the Administrator's Executive Council, which, pretty soon, became known as "The Cabinet". The ten nominated for membership included the five leading Pangu Pati members, Somare, Kiki, Olewale, Lapun and Taureka; Guise represented the independent group, and Kavali and Okuk the National Party; the PPP representatives were Chan and Mola. The AEC also had three official members, Newman, the Deputy Administrator, Kearney, the Secretary for Law, and Harry Ritchie, the new Treasurer. Ritchie had replaced a namesake, Jim Ritchie, who had just accepted the post of Deputy Vice-Chancellor at the University of Queensland. I was Chairman of the whole shooting match.

The portfolios allotted to the Ministers who were AEC members were:

Iambakey Okuk	Agriculture, Stock and Fisheries	(NP)
Donatus Mola	Business Development	(PPP)
Ebia Olewale	Education	(Pangu)
Reupena Taureka	Health	(Pangu)
John Guise	Interior	(Independent)
Julius Chan	Internal Finance	(PPP)
Albert Maori Kiki	Lands and Environment	(Pangu)
Paul Lapun	Mines	(Pangu)
Thomas Kavali	Works	(NP)

The outer Ministry comprised:

| Sasakila Moses | Forests | (NP) |
| Paulus Arek | Information | (Independent) |

Gavera Rea	Labour	(Pangu)
Boyamo Sali	Local Government	(Pangu)
Kaibelt Diria	Posts and Telegraphs	(NP)
John Poe	Trade and Industry	(PPP)
Bruce Jephcott	Transport	(PPP)

Meanwhile in the House there was turmoil. The United Party was shell-shocked. It was by far the largest party, but on the first day of the first meeting of the third House of Assembly it found all of its members excluded from government. The weekend did nothing to assuage their pain and they turned up on Monday morning determined to give their victorious opponents a rough time. Tei Abal, the appointed leader of the UP, led the charge: "All the people of Papua New Guinea do not accept the formation of the coalition government which was only formed last week. The United Party also does not think that this is correct. This is a dummy government. The people of Papua New Guinea do not agree with the new Government. . . . When the new Ministry is announced by the coalition the United Party will do its best to throw it out."[3]

He was strongly supported by Matiabe Yuwi, a tough and intelligent man from a remote part of the Southern Highlands. Yuwi had been the target for blandishment from the coalition because he was a deal more open-minded than some of his highlands colleagues. "Whoever tries to talk me into joining his party will never convince me. I am very surprised that their sweet talk has already won over a lot of members. Such members are not true leaders of their people."[4]

But the principal target for personal attack by UP members was their erstwhile member Kaibelt Diria. When he spoke he was subjected to a barrage of hostile interjections which the new and totally inexperienced Speaker was quite unable to control.[5] The Hansard record has converted into polite English a great many very impolite phrases spoken in the original Pidgin. The place was a bear garden. An early luncheon break terminated these preliminary hostilities.

After lunch Michael Somare made a creditable attempt to secure tolerance if not acceptance of the situation with a speech offering something to all sections of the community.

> Our coalition is a national coalition. Some honourable members are not in our coalition. I would like to assure these honourable members that this will not mean that their people will be overlooked by this coalition. We aim for fair distribution of government activities regardless of political affiliations. . . . I would like to assure the businessmen of this country that our coalition is pro-businessmen . . . and this coalition is a truly multiracial one. . . . The coalition accepts the People's Progress Party's platform that the timing of self-government is not as important as the type of self-government best suited for this country. . . .
>
> I am going to arrange certain facilities for the leader of the Opposition, including a special salary and also some support staff so that he can carry out his job well.[6]

The House settled down a bit with other speakers being less rancorous. John Guise was positively statesmanlike, advocating, once again, consideration of a quasi-Presidential form of government. Donatus Mola, the only Bougainville member not committed to separatism, was also a moderating influence. "Self-government will neither bring immediate wealth to a country, nor will it bring revolution and bloodshed. If we have self-government we will continue to live on sweet potatoes and coconuts. It does not mean that we will be in danger."[7]

Opposition was in a lower key when Somare presented his ministerial list to the House on 26 April, after surviving an attempt by the opposition to defer the appointments — "further actions on the appoint-

Matt Toliman is invested with the C.B.E.

ment of Ministers should be delayed until members can consult their electorates on their opinion of immediate self-government".[8] The opposition could only muster forty-two votes in support as against fifty-four for the National Coalition. Thereafter resistance evaported.

Toliman commented: "Mr Somare is often my political enemy but socially he is a good friend of mine. I wish him well. However, I am sorry not to see a Tolai in the Ministry."[9] However, Tei Abal, in congratulating Somare, fired a shot or two across his bows: "I would like the leader of the Coalition Government to be well aware of several things which are urgently needed at this stage such as the balanced development of the country of Papua New Guinea and the appointment and distribution of work to all the people in this country . . . appointments and promotions in the Public Service must be representational of all regions of the country . . . I give this warning because my people from the Highlands have previously been forgotten and this might lead to trouble in the country."[10] Oscar Tammur also put in a word for his fellow Tolais, or perhaps for himself. "You might ask What about the Tolais? Why has one of them not been given a portfolio?"[11]

The actual allocation of portfolios to the new Ministers were presented to the House on 28 April and this time aroused no opposition at all. Thereafter for the remainder of the brief first meeting members returned to their more usual preoccupations of seeing what could be done to remedy the deficiencies in their electorates, and the new Government got the membership of its parliamentary committees organized, giving appropriate representation to opposition members. The first meeting concluded with the coalition numbers firm while a demoralized opposition had grudgingly accepted defeat. Now the real business of government would begin — the translation of policies into practice, the facing up to difficult decisions and accepting responsibility for them. The National Coalition Government was off, but not yet running.

26 April, 1972

M.T. Somare Esq. MHA
House of Assembly
PORT MORESBY

Dear Mr Somare,

On the assumption that the House of Assembly endorses the Ministerial list we have agreed upon, I hope that we may proceed to the election of the Deputy Chairman of the AEC on Thursday morning, 27 April. I will today give notice to Ministers of this meeting.

The constitutional position as per the *Papua New Guinea Act* section 20 (i) (c) is that Ministers are then appointed to portfolios and the nine places in the AEC by the Minister for External Territories on the nomination of the Administrator, after consultation with the Deputy Chairman.

Let me say right away that I have no intention of disputing AEC membership. I am happy to nominate for AEC membership those Ministers put forward by the Deputy Chairman. However, I am "charged with the duty of administering the government of the Territory on behalf of the Commonwealth" under section 13 of the *Papua New Guinea Act*, and I offer some comments on portfolio allocation for your consideration before we begin discussions.

In the first place I believe that it is a good principle to have the AEC Ministers responsible for the most important portfolios. This, of course, is not essential and there may be good reason to include in the AEC a man who by reasons of particular talents is best placed in charge of a relatively less important portfolio. But on the assumption that this latter circumstance is likely to be unusual, I list below those portfolios which I consider to be most important:

Lands
Education
Transport
Health
Agriculture
Internal Finance
Interior
Labour
Trade

Public Works is a technical service Department and has little involvement in major policy. I prefer Trade to Business Development because of the major role Trade plays in the important commodity agreements for coffee, cocoa and other agricultural products and for that Department's responsibility for attracting large-scale industrial development. Transport is vital for our whole development programme and involves planning for land, sea and air. Labour, in its influence on industrial relations and wages policy, is more significant than Mines, though Mines may assume increasing importance if there are additional significant mineral discoveries.

A second principle I put forward is that the most experienced and able Ministers should handle the most important portfolios. I think that it is sometimes a positive disadvantage for a Minister to have had a close inside knowledge of the Department he takes charge of. Inevitably he interferes with the internal management of the Department, which is the business of the Director. The Minister's task is to guide policy and ensure that his Department's actions conform to political realities. He is concerned with broad issues and not departmental minutiae. A Minister who has worked as a member of a department too is subject to pressures from those with whom he has worked and may well have developed personal prejudices and antipathies that may render him less than dispassionate in his guidance of that department. If a Minister is able, there is much to be said for appointing an outsider to a particular portfolio so that new points of view may be injected into the Department's thinking.

In my view, the Ministries of greatest importance after the position of Deputy Chairman are those of Lands, Internal Finance, Education and Agriculture. I would hope that you would suggest men of special abilities to fill these posts.

Lands require a man who will have to make some tough decisions and risk unpopularity for the good of his country. Agriculture is presently in a state of depression and important policy decisions on assistance proposals will need early consideration. Education has the biggest share of our budget and holds the key to our future. The importance of Internal Finance is self-evident.

I look forward to substantive discussion on portfolios as soon as the Ministry has elected the Deputy Chairman.

Yours sincerely,

(L.W. Johnson)
ADMINISTRATOR

NOTES

1. *Papua New Guinea*, Woolford, University of Queensland Press, 1976.
2. Notes dictated 26 March 1972, PP.
3. P.N.G., House of Assembly Debates (HAD), vol. III, no. 1, p. 12.
4. Ibid., p. 14.
5. Kwan proved to be an inept Speaker and was replaced during the second meeting by Barry Holloway, an Australian, who was a foundation member of the Pangu Pati.
6. P.N.G., HAD, vol. III, no. 1, p. 22.
7. Ibid., p. 43.
8. Ibid., pp. 48–56.
9. Ibid., p. 58.
10. Ibid., p. 60.
11. Ibid.

8

TAKING UP THE REINS

I dictated an account of the first meeting of the AEC on the day following its conclusion. Here it is:

The new AEC met for the first time on 2 May. On the preceding day all Ministers met with me and we had a general discussion about the power of Ministers, the conventions of Cabinet loyalty, the relationships with departmental heads, with public servants and with fellow MHAs. Paul Ryan explained salary and allowance entitlements, housing, etc. and Thos Barnett gave an account of the preparations for self-government, the major tasks to be undertaken and the nature and extent of final powers of Ministers. Then all departmental heads came in and we concluded the day with a few drinks.

On the Tuesday, the AEC meeting began at 9.00 a.m. with everyone present and punctual, Somare on my right and Guise on my left. Official members took their places modestly at the end of the table. As the first ten minutes of the meeting were being filmed we occupied it with an outline of the procedures the previous AEC had adopted, the general desirability of reaching agreed decisions rather than by majority vote and the freedom to use either English or Pidgin according to choice. All members understood both languages though some speak only one of them with fluency.

The first real business of the day was the choice of

representatives for the UN Trusteeship Council and for the South Pacific Cultural Festival in Fiji. For the former, Gavera Rea had been pre-selected and Somare had rather rashly promised the second berth to a freshman MHA from the Chimbu District. The Council was not about to have this and Guise immediately raised the problem that this would mean two votes off the floor of the House for the June meeting. He proposed Neville on the basis that it was Neville's third term in the House, during which time he had not had any overseas excursions and that it would equalize voting. Not unexpectedly, there were some demurs and a decision was adjourned until the next day. However, ultimately it was decided that Neville should be first choice and if he was unable to go, then I was to consult with available Ministers to choose a suitable UP representative. Parao, Langro and Yuwi were mentioned. It was interesting to note the individual antipathies. Somare would not have Langro, Kavali would not have Parao and Kiki would not have Neville. To finish the story — Parao finally accompanied the party, which was made up of Rea and Parao with two accompanying public servants, Pearsall and Kaumi.

Knowing of Somare's discomforture because of his promise to the Chimbu member, John Kaupa, I suggested in an aside that we should add him to the Fiji expedition and this was done later in the meeting. Kaupa himself, when brought to Moresby, was surprised to find that he was going to Fiji as he said that he had been busy preparing his speech to the UN. Perhaps it was fortunate that he did not get a chance to deliver it.

As to the Fiji party, I had thought that Guise would represent us. Although most Heads of States in the South Pacific were attending, it was clearly impossible for Somare to go and in earlier discussions with Pangu Pati officials I had understood that they would be happy to have Guise out of the way for a while. Whether they changed their minds or whether Somare handled it maladroitly or Guise himself decided against it I do not know, but Taureka, who has a Fijian wife, was nominated. Taureka intimated rather coyly that he would be prepared to serve his country in this capacity.

The main business of the meeting was to acquaint them with the budget plan for 1972/73 so that the leadership group could importune the Commonwealth Treasurer in an appropriate manner. We presented the figures in as simple a form as possible but to any group of newcomers they would be overwhelming and it was not surprising that Ministers were groping to comprehend them. However, Chan applied himself to his task of Minister for Finance assiduously and got the hang of things fairly well. Lively discussion did develop over the matter of additional revenue and a number of spontaneous proposals were put forward:

Guise — an extra tax on all incomes over $10,000
Kiki — a national lottery
Olewale — a tax on betting.
Additional petrol tax was also suggested.

No decisions were made. At a later meeting of the Finance, Works and Planning Committee a decision was made to start discussions in Canberra on the basis of no additional internal revenue measures for 1972/73 but a request that an additional Commonwealth grant fill the existing gap of $13 million. Such completely unrealistic expectations were to be expected at this stage of development. It was decided that the full Finance Committee should visit Canberra — Somare, Guise, Chan, Kavali and Olewale — and that a retinue of experts should accompany them — McCasker, Milne and Douglas. External Territories were somewhat taken aback by this decision and will be reluctant hosts to an invasion of this magnitude.

The surplus funds thrown up by the third quarter budget review for 1971/72 was also discussed with the unusual task of finding a home for an unexpected $3 million. Allocations made were: as much additional funds into housing as could be spent in the remainder of the financial year; $1 million into the sinking funds against the expectation that payments to the Copra Stabilization Fund would continue at a high level in the next financial year, and the balance into the Investment Corporation. There are some surprising gaps in the knowledge of our new Ministers. Kiki knew nothing of the Investment Corporation and had to have the whole thing explained to him.

A surprise was the enthusiasm displayed for the "Build and buy back" office proposal for the new City Centre in the Waigani valley. I had expected some opposition on the grounds of quality and cost, but all seemed to agree that a good quality building to house the larger departments was highly desirable, for most departments are still housed in temporary war-time buildings that were little better than shacks. The Department of Home Affairs was authorized to proceed with negotiations.

There were reasonable participation of Ministers in discussions. Okuk did not have much to say and Kavali had some difficulty in following the English which was used most of the time. Guise, as ever, demonstrated his strongly individualistic views.

That evening I made a broadcast over all Papua New Guinea radio stations to outline in simple terms the new situation, using some metaphorical allusions, a common way of communicating ideas in Papua New Guinea.

Part of the text of the broadcast is given here:

The AEC makes decisions about the government of Papua New Guinea that are very important to all of us, decisions about schools, roads, hospitals, taxes and many other things. But the AEC cannot do these things against the wishes of the House of Assembly. The people you elected to be Members are there to ensure that Ministers and the AEC work for the good of all of the people of Papua New Guinea. . . .

The Ministers and the AEC are your government. They are there to try to make Papua New Guinea a better country for everyone. Sometimes you may not agree with their ideas. In this country you are free to say when you disagree. You are free to make known your own ideas and you have elected Members to let Ministers know how you feel about the matters that are important to you. When we do not agree in this country, if we are wise, we sit down together and discuss our differences and try to find a road on which we can travel together. We do not put logs across the road so that no one can go ahead. Let us then plan to sit down together to decide the road we should travel and let us go down this road together."[2]

Shortly thereafter the assertion of independence from the control of a white colonial bureaucracy came in the request for funds for Ministers to appoint advisers of their own choice. Tony Voutas, the Pangu Pati strategist, saw me about it and although I should not have been surprised it came as something of a shock that the party would want to hold itself at arms' length from the Administration departments. The request was for a staff of twelve political appointees for the Chief Minister and lesser numbers for the rest of the Ministry. It would have been tantamount to setting up an alternative administration. Nevertheless we bit on the bullet, but offered four instead of twelve staffers plus a Department staffed by Administration officers. It was initially called the Office of the Chief Minister. Somare accepted, and appointed Paul Cowdy, a journalist who was to be Press Secretary, John Yock Lunn, at the time the librarian at the Administrative College, and Tony and Christine Voutas. All were original stalwarts of the Pangu Pati. The group were sensible, intelligent persons with whom I was sure we could work, and in fact the relationship between the Chief Minister, his personal staff and the Public Service department of the Chief Minister was always harmonious. We agreed on two staff members for each other Minister. I was rather less happy about individual Ministers selecting their support and we held down the classification of these personal private secretaries so that it would not be too attractive to fortune hunters. There was also potential trouble if the Ministers selected a disgruntled public servant who could, and sometimes did, set himself up in opposition to his erstwhile departmental head. Guise chose only Papua New Guinean staffers but one or two Ministers made grossly inept choices — one selected a criminal, one or two chose attractive young Australian women whose talents were not of a political nature; but on the whole we survived, as indeed did the Public Service in Australia a few months later when shocked by the influx of private advisers to the new Labor Government. As Ministers grew in sophistication and understanding their choice of advisers improved, though there remained one or two cases when emotion overrode other factors. Some U.S. Senators also seem not immune to this failing.

The Department of the Chief Minister was a new creation to provide the necessary bureaucratic support. It consisted of three divisions.

1. The Ministerial Services Division, which would act as a link between the Chief Minister's personal staff and the Public Service as a whole and also provide research and other supporting services. It was headed up by Leo Morgan, a Bougainvillean and a graduate of the University of Papua New Guinea.
2. The Cabinet Secretariat, which would provide service and support for the AEC. Mark Lynch, a young Australian, was in charge.
3. The Political Development Division, which would handle all planning for the transition to self-government. Thos Barnett, a young lawyer, was its chief.

Paul Ryan was the overall director. Somare had agreed to the appointments and I was confident we had a very good team. They were experienced but young and forward-looking, in tune with the political developments taking place. They played a very important part in the relatively smooth transition to self-government and independence over the next few years.

In early May, at the request of the Minister for External Territories I summarized the situation as it appeared to me. Rather protracted excerpts follow. It seemed to me the best way of indicating how we, in Papua New Guinea, saw things at that time.

You are familiar with the developments which have produced a coalition group which commands a majority in the House of Assembly, currently about 54 or 55 votes of the 99 elected members on the floor of the House. I think this support is likely to be maintained or even increased unless the People's Progress Party finds that it is being drawn into measures contrary to its policies. There is no doubt that the dominant partner is the Pangu Pati and that this party will be active and vigorous in promoting its policies. It has a strong extra-parliamentary group and it can be expected that from these party advisers, a positive programme of legislation will emanate, some of it probably ill-considered, and that the existing restraints of Commonwealth controls will be cast off as soon as practicable. How soon this might be, is discussed further below.

Opinion is likely to move more strongly in the direction of self-government and any attempts by the Commonwealth to influence legislation which it might not favour will be resented and possibly diminish Australian influence in the longer term.

The public attitude of the coalition towards self-government was set out by Mr Somare in his first speech to the new parliament. In effect the coalition accepted the People's Progress Party's policy in this matter. I think that there is no doubt at all that most of the supporters of the coalition, with the exception of course of PPP, do not accept it and will work to achieve a parliamentary majority which will permit them to fulfil their policy of early self-government. However, I believe that the party leadership now recognizes that there are some substantial obstacles to be overcome before all of the requirements of a self-governing Papua New Guinea can be met. The party may be satisfied with a large degree of de facto self-government if this is conceded at a reasonably early date while the larger obstacles are being overcome.

However, I have this week discussed with Mr Somare and Mr Chan the coalition attitude towards constitutional development. Mr Somare asserts that his statement in the House of Assembly is a proper reflection of the opinion of his followers at this point in time.

Both Mr Somare and Mr Chan agreed that the coalition would be satisfied to institute constitutional discussions with the Australian Government after the June meeting of the House of Assembly. They agreed that they understood the Australian Government's position that any further constitutional advances that might be agreed upon by the coalition and the Australian Government would need House of Assembly endorsement. I pointed out that this would mean that endorsement could not take place until August/September and that further action required by the Australian Government, such as amendment of the *Papua New Guinea Act* to increase the size of the Ministry, would probably be affected by the imminence of an Australian election. They said that they appreciated the nature of this difficulty.

The general expectations of the adherents to the coalition were then discussed and I set out below what seemed to be an agreed position between the two leaders, though there could be no assurance the party members would support it.

Arising from the July meeting with the Australian Government and subsequent House of Assembly endorsement, there could be extension of Ministerial final powers in portfolios already held and up to three new Ministries created. Two that have been specifically mentioned are Economic Planning and Urban Development. Given the likely long delays in amending the *Papua New Guinea Act* to create additional Ministries, it might be possible to appoint some MHAs as "Members assisting the Minister of . . . " and means of providing special allowances for these will be investigated.

Up to the present there has been no mention of assuming powers in such sensitive areas as Internal Security but I believe that a July meeting should plan for this during 1973 on the basis of delegation of powers as was previously discussed. The larger problems of achieving total self-government was referred to briefly: e.g.
- long-term financial arrangements with the Commonwealth;
- Banking;

- Department of Civil Aviation;
- and others.

There is at present no obvious intention of the coalition, or of the Pangu Pati for that matter, to rush its fences but it will have to show its members substantial actual progress towards its self-government objective at an early date with longer term plans also outlined. The People's Progress Party through its leader is much more cautious but may find it difficult to act as an effective brake.

Might I suggest that the Australian Government consider the following broad timetable:

Stage I

Notionally
July/December 1972
1. An agreed definition of self-government.
2. Extension of final powers of Ministers in existing portfolios.
3. Creation of new Ministries with final powers in areas outside of those considered sensitive, e.g. exclude Internal Security and Law.
4. Initiate planning for orderly transmission of powers in sensitive areas and agree upon an approximate timetable.
5. Arising out of current planning for the development of a Department of Law with a Papua New Guinean Minister exercising final powers, the initial drafting of legislation to insulate from political pressures Crown Solicitor, Public Prosecutor and Electoral Office.
6. Consideration of changing role and powers of Administrator.
7. Commence border negotiations; P.N.G./Indonesia : P.N.G./Australia.
8. Establishment of Constitutional Commission.

Stage II

1. Delegation of Police and other internal security powers.

2. Commence substantive discussion on Defence arrangements.
3. Passage of legislation referred to in Stage I.

Stage III

1. Consideration of recommendations of Constitutional Commission.
2. Banking legislation — currency.
3. Local control of Public Service Board.
4. Finalization of borders negotiations.

Stage IV

1. Implementation of agreed recommendations of Constitutional Commission.
2. Final legislation for complete self-government.

I appreciate that the "gearing up" programme takes account of all eventualities and in the above outline I have confined myself to the issues which are of direct significance to the exercise of effective self-government.[3]

In succeeding meetings of the AEC some members began to assert themselves, to exhibit a good grasp of their portfolios and to come up with thoughtful contributions to overall policy deliberations. Apart from the Chief Minister, Somare, those who come most readily to mind are John Guise, the veteran politician, Albert Maori Kiki, one of the creators of the Pangu Pati, Julius Chan, the founder of the PPP and Iambakey Okuk, a Chimbu member of the National Party.

Perhaps the most original mind was Okuk's. He was previously a motor mechanic and was then aged twenty-eight. He was strongly antagonistic towards expatriates in general and was probably the most radical Minister. Otherwise he was not constrained by preconceived ideas and brought a good mind to bear upon his government's problems. He was not about to be restrained in developing his ideas and had some spirited clashes with his expatriate departmental officers. Kiki was the most reliable supporter of the Chief Minister, and his strength of character kept a somewhat heterogenous group together. Chan, by virtue of a sound education and a good deal of successful business experience, had a better grasp of the issues and a more orthodox approach to dealing with them. He was quite at home with the expatriate Treasury officials and his was the most successful fusion of a new Minister with his department. John Guise, as befitted his long political career, was the most positive of his colleagues, but was isolated within the Council because his fellows were always a bit doubtful of his intentions. Obviously his long-term ambition was to lead his country and there was some apprehension that he might do a deal with the opposition to achieve his ambition. He was the most autocratic of Ministers so far as his Department was concerned, which led to some confrontations with his very determined departmental head, David Fenbury. The two men, however, were the oldest of friends and harmony was usually restored eventually.

The advent of the NCG certainly changed the nature of government in Papua New Guinea, and as might well be expected there were growing pains. Previously the loose accretion of UP members with parochial preoccupations and with no defined self-government objectives had left policy initiatives in the hands of expatriate officials. Now, in May 1972, there was a Government fuelled by Pangu Pati concepts and with some firm objectives, the most positive, at this time, being that of early self-government. Pangu was suspicious of its white public servants and, given the inexperience and relative lack of education of its Ministers, had reason to be cautious in dealing with them. There is no doubt that senior public servants would have cheerfully continued to dominate government activities and to manage the country's affairs. If the politicians were to assert themselves they had to consult other sources of advice. In concept the idea was sound enough, but in practice it made for difficulties due to paucity of suitable advisers, though there was an abundance of aspirants. As mentioned previously, some Ministers made grossly inappropriate choices, while others benefited greatly from the advice of original and inventive thinkers such as Ross Garnaut, who assisted Julius Chan.

However, public servants in some Departments faced resistance to their advice to Ministers on illogical grounds, and had to endure erratic and irresponsible intervention by ministerial advisers. In this situation some of the expatriates adopted passivity as their defence and simply awaited direction and initiative from their new masters. When this failed to eventuate activity began to run down, previously energetic and busy men vegetated and spent their days calculating what their redundancy compensation payment would be and when they would get it. Job satisfaction decreased dramatically, and those who had faced the prospect of early self-government and independence with doubts and fears began to look forward to it as a time of release.

The above criticism obviously did not apply to all. Many expatriate public servants felt genuinely that the time had come for Papua New Guineans to make their own decisions and accept responsibility for them, and the only way that this could be accomplished was for the public servant to withdraw from taking initiatives himself. However, thrust rather too rapidly into positions of executive authority, many Papua New Guineans were not sure enough of their roles, or their competence to direct. A further negative factor was the mass of ministerial statements, usually emanating from advisers, highly critical of past actions and policies, and promising a new world tomorrow.

Of course new governments are always critical of their predecessors but soon find that the task of shifting the cumbersome government machine on to a new track is neither a quick nor an easy task. Apart from the straightforward objective of early self-government, the evolution of new social and economic policies was a painful and protracted process. Essentially there was a strong commitment to uniform development and a somewhat optimistic expectation that less emphasis on economic growth would, somehow or other, result in better conditions for those living in depressed areas. The only implementation of such a policy came sixteen months after the NCG assumed office and then it was no more than doubling a grant for subsidies to local government councils for development projects.

The coalition Ministry soon found that government was a good deal more than having the numbers in parliament and issuing statements.

NOTES

1. Memo, PP.
2. Record of speech, PP.
3. Summary, PP.

9

ACTION AND INACTION

The first priority for the Pangu Pati, though perhaps not for its coalition partner, the PPP, was to get House of Assembly endorsement for a date for self-government. The Australian Government was also eager to have a target date, but let it be known that it would expect a substantial majority in the House to support the date put forward by the Papua New Guinea Government, and that majority would need to be broadly representative of the whole of Papua New Guinea.[1] Somare wasted no time in getting down to business. He tabled a paper on self-government at the June meeting of the House[2] and after due time for the digestion of its contents, moved its adoption at the third meeting in September. In full, the motion read:

> That the House take note of the paper and (a) requests that constitutional changes necessary for full internal self-government be brought into effect on 1 December 1973, or as soon as possible thereafter; (b) interprets full internal self-government for Papua New Guinea as leaving with the Commonwealth of Australia final powers only in the matters of defence and external affairs, which it should exercise in the fullest consultation with the Government of Papua New Guinea.[3]

The United Party had also considered a self-government date previously and had reached agreement for December 1975, which was a considerable advance on their pre-election thinking, despite the second House's conditional acceptance of a date during the life of the third House, that is, before 1976.

The coalition government was worried that support for December 1973 might not be sufficient to qualify as "a substantial majority broadly representative of the whole of Papua New Guinea" and Somare would have been prepared to move backwards a bit to broaden support had there been an organized resistance to his proposal. As it was, there was a great deal of rhetoric but little substance in a protracted, and, at times, an acrimonious debate. Nor were there any attempts to amend the motion. Anton Parao, one of the younger highland members of the UP, got nearest to the bone; "I do not want to see the white colonial government handed to a black colonial government just for the sake of a small minority group such as Mr Michael Somare's Government."[4]

Somare responded "It is high time that the people of this country held their heads high . . . and have pride in their country. If not now, when?"[5] Eventually came the division and Somare's motion was accepted fifty-two votes to thirty-four. We white colonials and our Minister in Canberra debated whether or not this majority fulfilled our self-imposed criteria. I canvassed the voting pattern with the Secretary of the Department of External Territories and estimated the allegiances of the thirteen absent from the division, (the Speaker did not vote).

Of the total House voting strengths of 99 members, 56 were certain supporters, 35 were certain opponents, 4 absentees were possible supporters and 4 absentees were doubtful. You will note that voters in favour of the motion came from all districts except the Southern Highlands where there were absentees who were potential supporters. A summary of the regional distribution follow:

	Ayes	Noes	Absent
N.G. Islands	13	2	2
N.G. Coast	20	6	2
Papua	12	3	3
Highlands	7	23	6
Total	52	34	13 [6]

We came to the conclusion that the numbers and their distribution were enough, and although the 1 December date was qualified by the phrase "or as soon as possible thereafter" everybody knew that 1 December was to be self-government day. We had our target date at last and the colonial administration was on its way out.

Somare was jubilant, the major plank in the Pangu Pati's platform, early self-government, was close to achievement, but in other respects the necessity to maintain a policy consensus with the party's ill-assorted coalition partners was frustrating. In particular, the tendency of individuals within the coalition to proclaim their own personal views on important issues was a continuing embarrassment. The September meeting of the House provided a number of examples of this.

The Minister for Mines, the Bougainvillean Paul Lapun, was sought out and interviewed on the ABC radio programme "Contact", and his well known antipathy to large scale mining ventures by foreign mining companies on his own patch were extracted from him through the application of a series of leading questions. Lapun, in attempting to clarify his views, only succeeded in creating greater alarm in the breasts of the mining magnates but persisted in the naive belief that public statements made on mining by Paul Lapun, the member for Bougainville, did not reflect the views of the Government of which Paul Lapun was Minister for Mines. Bruce Jephcott seemed to have the same sort of faith in a series of contradictory statements about airline policy, all related to a very precise and detailed statement of Government policy on the establishment of a single airline publicized by the Chief Minister and the Australian Minister for Civil Aviation which was produced after a series of consultations in which Jephcott participated and had indicated his firm concurrence.

The mining issue was further complicated by the introduction of a long and detailed resolution by John Momis, the member for Bougainville Regional. Coming from a member of the Government party it seemed to be either a declaration of personal faith or an attempt to take the running away from his own government. I expressed my concern in a letter to the Chief Minister:

> I am particularly concerned at the number of recent statements which will be widely regarded as defining Government policy in mining, whereas there has, as yet, been no careful delineation of Papua New Guinea's attitude towards future mineral development. I note, too, a detailed resolution on mining for the consideration of the House of Assembly proposed by a Government supporter which seems to me to be designed to take mining policy consideration out of the hands of the Government. If indeed the House should be involved closely in this matter it would be better to establish a Select Committee which could give more attention to it than the passing consideration of a House debate.[7]

In an attempt at clarification the Chief Minister, at a press conference, made the point that the Government had not yet given any consideration to mining policy, and in particular had not discussed the possible renegotiation of the agreement with the Bougainville mining company (Bougainville Copper), but he did opine that any newly independent government would be likely to re-examine agreements entered into by its colonial predecessor. This did little to lower the temperature of major investors in Papua New Guinea resources.

On another front, in the September meeting, the Chief Minister made an important statement on the Government's intention to reduce sharply the number of expatriates in the Public Service to a figure approaching 3000, by a fifteen per cent reduction in each of the next three years. The anxiety among expatriate public servants occasioned by this statement was soon to be relieved by the Australian Government's acceptance of the generous compensation scheme for displaced white officers.

Somare again enunciated his party's policy on equality:

> Economic development under my Government will be directed at a more even sharing of wealth between expatriate and national, between rich Papua New Guineans and poor Papua New Guineans, and between districts. I do not want to see a very rich black elite emerge here at the expense of village people. I do not want government activity to be directed at satisfying the demands of a black elite. My Government will always regard ordinary people as being the most important people in the country.[8]

But the National Coalition Government did not always speak with one voice, in particular the Pangu Pati and the People's Progress Party were somewhat uneasy partners. In fact, PPP as a supporter of private enterprise, small businesses and overseas investment, had little in common with the Pangu Pati quasi-socialist philosophy. In the initial euphoria of winning the Government benches the Pangu Pati had overlooked the need to ensure control of the Departments responsible for economic development, despite some advice to the contrary, and the PPP had demanded and got Treasury, Trade, Business Development and Transport. Chan, the leader of the PPP, with a good educational background and some business experience, was certainly the best suited for the Finance portfolio and, aided and abetted by young Treasury officers, proceeded to make his portfolio into a major base.

On the other hand, the Chief Minister's personal advisers, in fact the Pangu Pati expatriate executive, wished to take their own financial policy initiatives. It was plain that there would be clashes. AEC meetings saw a number of disagreements on investment policy and other matters not primarily Treasury functions but certainly ones with significant finance interests, but the major disagreements arose over development planning policy and control of planning machinery. The responsibility for planning lay with the Office of Planning and Co-ordination. It was originally directly responsible to the Administrator, and at this time was gearing up to design Papua New Guinea's second five-year-plan to cover the period 1973–78.

The Chief Minister and his advisers were determined that the Office of Planning and Co-ordination should not fall into the hands of the petit bourgeoisie of the PPP, while Chan and his supporters were equally intent on preserving their influence on development planning.

The Chief Minister's office first presented a policy economic development paper for Cabinet consideration containing a good many vague generalizations and not departing too far from previous objectives, though those responsible seemed to be under the impression that it indicated a complete change of direction. Chan's supporters countered with a paper rather more definite in specific objectives which he called an improvement plan rather than a development plan. Both papers were circulated by the respective groups among Ministers and Departments with requests for comments.

These tactics effectively delayed formal Cabinet consideration of development policy for two or three months and meanwhile the struggle developed for the control of planning machinery. The impasse was eventually resolved by a compromise which had little to recommend it. The existing office was dismembered with its constituent parts being divided between the rival groups, but with the core retained and made responsible to a Cabinet sub-committee comprising the coalition leaders, Somare, Guise, Chan and Kavali, a group in which Chan would be isolated. Meanwhile time had passed so that 1973–74, for planning purposes, had to become an interim year with the long-term five-year-plan to span the years 1974–79. Chan may have derived some minor satisfaction from the fact that the plan was now to be called the Improvement Programme.

Meanwhile the House of Assembly was slugging it out over the Annual Appropriation Bills, debate centering but rarely on national issues, as members, as in the past, took the opportunity to impress on the Government the urgent needs of their electorates for roads, bridges, schools health services and so on. But the Government got through the session relatively unscathed. As well as the decision on the date for self-government, another important matter to reach finality during the meeting was to set up a Constitutional Planning Committee and to establish its terms of reference and its membership. It was a successor to the committees of the first and second Houses of Assembly. The task of this third one was a deal more fundamental. Somare, introducing the motion to set up the Committee, said it is important that the fullest consideration be given to the type of future government we shall have. It is for our people that a constitution will be made. It is our people who shall have to live under the system of government that is established. We must ensure, therefore, that the constitution is suited to the needs and circumstances of Papua New Guinea and is not imposed from outside. In short it should be a home-grown constitution.[9]

The terms of reference proposed, and accepted, for the Committee were sweeping in the extreme, and I was concerned at the latitude given, for, although Somare had appointed himself as Chairman, he did not plan to play an active part. The real leader of the Committee would be the deputy Chairman, John Momis, a man of determination with fixed views. However, I refrained from comment, deeming that P.N.G.'s independence Constitution was not the business of the colonial Administrator. The terms of reference, tabled in the House by Somare, were as follows:

To make recommendations for a constitution for full internal self-government in a united Papua New Guinea with a view to eventual independence. Without limiting the power of the Committee to make any investigation or recommendation which it deems relative to the objective, matters to be considered by the committee for possible incorporation into the constitution or related documents should include the following:
(a) the system of government: executive, legislature and judiciary;
(b) central-regional-local government relations and district administration;
(c) relations with Australia;
(d) defence and external affairs — transitional provisions;
(e) the machinery of government — control, organization and structure of the Public Service;
(f) a Director of Public Prosecutors and a Public Solicitor;

(g) an ombudsman and tribunals of administrative review;
(h) protection of minority rights;
(i) a Bill of Rights;
(j) emergency powers;
(k) citizenship;
(l) procedure for amendment of the constitution; and
(m) judicial review — the power of a court to decide whether or not any action by the Government or, law passed by parliament is in accordance with the constitution.

In addition, the Committee should be asked to consider the mechanism for implementing the constitution, including the possibility of holding a constitutional convention, and to make recommendations.

The Committee will be served by its own executive, legal, secretariat and consultant staff, all of whom will be solely responsible to the Committee.[10]

In terms of membership it was a strong committee:

Michael Somare	Chairman *ex officio*
John Momis	Deputy Chairman
John Guise	
John Kaputin	
John Kaupa	
Mackenzie Daugi	
Matiabe Yuwi	
Paul Langro	
Paulus Arek	
Pikah Kasau	
Sinake Giregire	
Stanis Toliman	
Tei Abal	
Tony Ila	

It had an abundance of professional support, but all the consultants, with the exception of the Papua New Guinean executive officer, Seaea Avosa, were from academic circles with little or no administrative experience. They included Professor Davidson from the Australian National University who had had a hand in constitution-making in Western Samoa, the Cook Islands, Nauru and Micronesia. Two complete outsiders were to be periodic consultants; Professor Ghai, formerly a professor of law in Tanzania, and Professor Mazrui, then a professor of political science at Makerere University in Uganda. Altogether, it was a formidable team likely both to wish, and be able, to wag the dog quite vigorously. In my view it was a major miscalculation of the Chief Minister and his advisers to surrender control of this most important committee to those who would most certainly have leadership ambitions of their own, and who would certainly exercise to the full the interventionist powers that the terms of reference gave them; which indeed they did.

I suppose that, given the number of mavericks among the members of the committee, it had looked a secure operation. Somare thought there was unlikely to be sufficient unity among the members to obstruct his own objective, a quick and controversy-free movement to self-government and independence; but, in fact, the Committee escaped his control entirely in the face of an alliance between Momis and Kaputin, the two best educated and most radical members of the team. The lack of interest of Guise and the death of Arek, the Chairmen of the two previous Constitutional Committees, both men who could have influenced the direction of events, left leadership in the hands of the radicals. Somare almost never attended meetings and the attendance of other members was erratic. The Constitutional Planning Committee (the CPC) became a consistent obstacle to the objectives of Somare and the Australian Government, both of whom wanted to hasten the movement to self government, while the CPC was intent on ensuring that Papua New Guinea's future system of government would not be cast in a colonial mould. The Committee was supported in its efforts by its variegated and somewhat amateur bunch of support staff and advisers.

The year 1972 was also the occasion for a pleasant ceremony when Papua New Guinea's largest town, Port Moresby, was proclaimed a city. The event took place on 13 April, and its Lord Mayor, Oala Oala Rarua, received congratulations all round, from supporters and opponents alike.

But the year also saw a major tragedy when a RAAF Caribou aircraft carrying twenty-five schoolboys who had been to an army cadet training camp crashed and killed the crew and twenty of the boys. It was some days before the crashed plane was located and the five survivors were rescued. Papua New Guinea was not unused to aircraft accidents but the magnitude of this

Port Moresby becomes a city; Oala Oala Rarua, the Lord Mayor, receives the City Charter, April 1972

one and the fact that the victims were the educated
youth so essential to Papua New Guinea's future cast a
gloom over the whole country. John Guise, the
Minister for the Interior, told the House of the tragedy.

> With great sorrow and sadness I have to announce to
> this House the result of the search for the RAAF
> Caribou which crashed while on a flight between Lae
> and Port Moresby on Monday last 28 August. It is
> evident that 24 of the 29 persons on board perished.
> These were the RAAF crew of three, an Australian
> army captain, an Army officer of cadets, 23 school
> cadels from De La Salle College, Bomana, and one
> school cadet from Popondetta High School. I have been
> advised that there were no survivors other than the five
> who were picked up yesterday. This has been a difficult
> operation because the aircraft crashed in exceptionally
> rough country. The aircraft is suspended in very tall
> timber on the edge of a ravine. . . . I offer my sorrow
> and I offer the sorrow and the sympathy of the Govern-
> ment to the relatives and friends. . . . If I may also do so
> I offer the sympathy and love of all the members of this
> House of Assembly for those who died in this tragic
> accident. Particularly in regard to the school cadets this
> country can ill afford to lose such fine young men, the
> cream of this country's manhood.[11]

For Papua New Guineans perhaps the most symbolic
action of the year was Somare's announcement, on 20
November, that a large proportion of the functions of
the Department of the Administrator were to be passed
over to the control of the Papua New Guinea Government, specifically to the Department of the Chief
Minister. The central one as far as Papua New Guinea
was concerned was control of District Administration,
which meant that all of those officers called "kiaps", and
including District Commissioners, would now be subject to the direction of their own elected government.

A few days later I reviewed, for the Minister of External Territories and the Department, the developments
and the problems as I saw them at the time:

House of Assembly

To date the NCG has not had any difficulty in maintaining a comfortable majority in divisions in the House but it has done this by sometimes swimming with the tide and acceding to House of Assembly motions which look to have popular support rather than asserting a Government policy and sticking to it. Outside Papua New Guinea, the internal politics of the House of Assembly are not well understood; nor the role played by private Members' motions in the House, by informal grouping of Members, by deals made and unmade by individual Ministers irrespective of earlier AEC decisions and by the strong influence of regional groupings.

Private Members' motions in the House of Assembly, even when supported by the ruling Coalition, are sometimes treated in a rather cavalier fashion when action on them is being considered by the AEC. Motions passed by the House are transmitted by the Speaker to the Administrator who refers them to the AEC for action. The usual timing is for a motion passed in one House meeting to be considered by the AEC after the conclusion of that meeting and a reply to the Speaker prepared for delivery during the next meeting. Subsequent action would then await any House reaction, although, of course, if there was full Cabinet support for the resolution, action could be initiated before the next meeting of the House. To date the House has not reacted strongly to a reasoned reply from the AEC which may, in fact, negate a House resolution which had been passed on the voices without opposition from any member of the Ministry. A number of Private Members' motions do impinge on the Government's prerogative to make policy but the NCG seems to be able to accept such motions without regarding policy implications as limiting its freedom of action.

The NCG does not act with consistent strength in the House of Assembly. There are occasions when it can and will muster its voting strength but these are usually when the United Party Opposition mounts a specific frontal attack. This means that jobs and influence are at risk and such threats rally the disparate elements within the NCG.

Much is said about consensus and, in a House in which there are no clear-cut ideological or economic divisions, perhaps broad agreement on principles without attempting to delineate specific issues is the best way to carry out parliamentary business. However, one should not be deluded into thinking that any Melanesian government will not act strongly and arbitrarily and, in so doing, override minority interests if it is confident it has the numbers and can get away with it.

Coalition solidarity

The Coalition has a high degree of fragility in that its principal elements — Pangu, People's Progress Party, Bougainvilleans and the Mataungan Association — have very little common ground. The cement that binds is the attraction of power and of office. On the face of it one might reasonably expect the defection of the PPP on many of the economic policy issues which are now coming to the surface, but I regard this as unlikely.

The Pangu Pati appears to have a high degree of flexibility on issues which may affect its control of government and, when it comes to the pinch, is likely to make concessions just sufficient to placate the PPP. The PPP also has only a small following, perhaps twelve or thirteen, some of whom may not be prepared to follow the party into opposition. The defection of the PPP, would certainly create political chaos and quite new groupings may emerge in which a more radical highlands group could play an important part.

The Ministry

As with all ministries everywhere, Papua New Guinea's is very uneven in capacity and understanding. It is handicapped by the fact that the best Ministers are not necessarily in charge of the more important portfolios and that some of the members of the AEC hold ministries of lesser importance. In general, Ministers arrive at Cabinet meetings poorly informed on the matters on the agenda and on very many occasions without having read the papers and without having attempted to get a briefing in any other way.

Because of political preoccupations and limited educational background, some Ministers rely very heavily on outside advice and assistance in matters relating to their portfolios and in certain cases, because of suspicion of a colonial and largely white senior public service, have been reluctant to accept departmental advice. Where extra-departmental advice is skilled and experienced, there are advantages in Ministers seeking this sort of help in addition to departmental aid, but some private advisers who have clustered around certain Ministers have neither knowledge nor experience. It will take some time for Ministers to exercise more perceptive judgment in selecting those who advise them.

A continuing problem throughout Papua New Guinea, both within and without the Government service, is the very limited number of people of high ability allied with experience and judgment.

The Opposition

The United Party Opposition has been ineffective for a number of reasons. The most obvious one is the dearth of Members with suitable education and experience and the fact that its principal strength lies in the Western and Southern Highlands Districts. Two of the more able and experienced Ministers from the previous House — Messrs Lokoloko and Giregire — have not taken an active part in politics in the present House and the remaining leaders of experience — Messrs Toliman and Abal — do not have the ruthlessness to develop strong attacks on the NCG. Two of the younger Members, Messrs Langro and Parao — have taken leading roles in attacks on the Government.

In general, the concept of a government and an opposition is weakly held. Mr Abal often says that he is opposed to the Pangu Pati but supports the NCG provided it manages the country's business properly. At present the actors in the House of Assembly appear to be frozen into Westminster postures which are unsuitable to their background, needs and aspirations. This makes for a good deal of aridity in set piece debates. The committee system has never been properly developed and the experiment of the British Solomon Islands in attempting to manage the Government through this system has apparently failed.

The Chief Minister

There has been a successful effort to build up the stature of the Chief Minister and to obtain acceptance of him as the national leader. The success obtained is due first of all to the personality and ability of Mr Somare and, second to the gratifying way in which senior public servants and private citizens everywhere have co-operated to present him to the nation as a leader.

Mr Somare has had a most onerous and difficult task in first of all mastering the business of government, holding together a difficult coalition and asserting himself in Cabinet. There is no credible alternative to Mr Somare on the horizon though there are two or three members of the National Coalition Government with sufficient ambition to attempt to supplant him should an occasion arise. In my judgment, the Coalition could not hold together for any length of time with any other leader.

Policy evolution

It might be said that the PPP supports a fairly orthodox capitalist approach to development while advocating greater equality of incomes and a wider geographic distribution of development spending. It favours a high level of foreign investment to maintain the rate of economic growth and to increase the number of jobs in towns. It advocates the maintenance of existing agree-

ments and contracts and protection of business interests
already operating here.

The Pangu Pati, insofar as it has a central policy
theme, advocates a much more socialist approach;
perhaps rural socialism might describe it best. The basis
of life in Papua New Guinea is the rural village and the
principal effort must be directed towards improving life
in the village. Economic growth per se has no merit nor
has foreign investment unless it can contribute to rural
improvement. It is suspicious of foreign capital. There is
a degree of unreality in its expectation of being able to
write its own terms for foreign investors and also for
international aid.

The Bougainvillean voice is principally that of Father
Momis who would chase the money changers out of the
temple and restore rural piety, purity and simplicity.

Out of these strands an economic policy must be
woven which the Australian Government is prepared
to support and which will go some way towards satisfying the demands for increased health and education services, more roads, improved agricultural extension services, improved security, more jobs in towns and so on.
This will entail some painful compromises but the
Pangu Pati is quite determined that it should be seen to
be changing direction. In the process it seems likely that
small scale foreign investors will find much less attraction in Papua New Guinea but the larger projects may
not be much affected if they act in conformity with
existing guidelines. However, intemperate statements
by individual Ministers and disinclination of the
Government as a whole to deny them have created a
climate of doubt and uncertainty in the boardrooms of
potential major investors, particularly mining and
mineral exploration companies. It will be some months
before there is sufficient definition of a Government investment policy to permit these companies to assess
Papua New Guinea opportunities.

Localization

Localization is an issue on which there is little difference between any political group and it was safe

enough for the Chief Minister to announce his Government's intention to reduce sharply the number of expatriates in the Public Service. It was politically necessary for him to use figures that would have some public impact and the Opposition expressed some concern that the baby might be thrown out with the bath water. The curious fact is that having made the announcement there appeared to be some reluctance to follow it through with action. Senior expatriates have been responsible for getting the project launched. The same reluctance has been evident in action to localize individual senior posts and, again, expatriate initiative has been necessary to get decisions.

The NCG has on a number of occasions asserted that it needs a simpler administrative structure and presently at least two proposals to reform departmental structure are in circulation. On the surface there is a readiness to impose radical solutions but little understanding of the difficulties facing any attempt at major reconstruction of an established and entrenched bureaucracy. There is already some evidence that senior indigenous public servants are closing ranks against the likely intrusion of politicians into managerial aspects of departmental business.

In both foreign policy and defence there has as yet been no discussion in depth and nothing more than the sporadic offering of tentative ideas. It is recognized that the major influences on Papua New Guinea will be Indonesia, Australia and Japan and Ministers appear to be groping towards a policy that will balance out the power and influence of these countries on Papua New Guinea. There is, in some quarters, a tendency to overreact against a long period of Australian paternalism but it seems that Australian ties will remain firm and enduring.

There is also a fraternal feeling for the other small Pacific nations and in particular towards those peopled by Melanesians but there is a ready appreciation that racial and cultural kinship does not do much to fill food bowls. One may confidently forecast the continuation of friendship and cultural and sporting contacts with the Pacific Island nations and perhaps some concerted action on any common political problems.

Internal security has not yet had serious consideration.

By far the greatest problem facing the National Coalition Government and one which is ever present in all
policy considerations, is the secessionist threat from
Bougainville. There is no doubt that at present Bougainville opinion is overwhelmingly secessionist, even
though few could explain precisely what they mean by
secession. The appointment of two Bougainvilleans to
Cabinet rank and a third to head up the Constitutional
Committee is an attempt to hold Bougainville by com-
mitting its parliamentary representatives to the Government of a united Papua New Guinea. The actions and
pronouncements of Bougainville MHAs receive exag-
gerated attention. A good example of this is the priority
attention given to Momis' successful attempt to set
mining policy for the Government. The Papua New
Guinea Government is playing for high stakes with a
weak hand and many of its actions and statements
which appear unreasonable are due to its anxiety about
Bougainville.

In general, the NCG has had first to overcome the
problem of political survival, next to obtain some
understanding of the business of government and, at
the same time, to build up public acceptance of
members of the Ministry as individuals and as a credible Government. It is only now beginning to evolve
policies which it hopes will be distinctively Papua New
Guinean.

Summary

I have not attempted to make final judgments on the
effectiveness of the NCG. It will require another six
months before any valid assessment can be made. In
that time the weaknesses and strengths of the Ministers
will become more apparent and we will have had a
view of policies, even if not of their implementation,
over a wide range of Government activities. It would
be idle to pretend that at present the Government is
working smoothly and efficiently, but the facts remain

that it is working, it is making its own decisions and it is surviving.[12]

The third House of Assembly concluded its third meeting on 28 November 1972. Oscar Tammur, still with us, had the last word.

> It would be an omission if the Government did not hear something from us terrible Mataungans. . . . We of the Mataungan Association are also happy with the coalition government. We support it and we co-operate with it. We would like to thank all our Ministers from the Chief Minister down. Our thanks also go to you Mr. Speaker, the Opposition and to all the other members. We Mataungan people are happy with all that has been done by this House. It is a fact that previously we Mataungan people were against the Government. Now the United Party is in opposition and we wicked Mataungan people are for the Government. We therefore extend our Christmas greetings to all our brothers. We are grateful that you are here and we look forward to next year when again we can bring forward our grievances. We Mataungan people therefore wish you all a happy Xmas and a happy New Year.[13]

NOTES

1. The agreed formula between the two governments was: "If a constitutional or important change is involved, both governments agree that there should be a recorded vote in favour, by a substantial majority of members, and that the majority should be broadly representative of the country".
2. P.N.G., House of Assembly Debates (HAD), vol. III, no. 2, p. 386.
3. P.N.G., HAD, vol. III, no. 6, p. 586.
4. Ibid., p. 574.
5. Ibid., p.587.
6. Administrator to Secretary, 22 September 1972, PP.
7. Letter, Administrator to Chief Minister, 28 September 1972, PP.
8. P.N.G., HAD, vol. III, no. 8, p. 871.

9. P.N.G., HAD, vol. IV, no. 2, p. 279.
10. Ibid., p. 280.
11. P.N.G., HAD, vol. III, no. 5, p. 510.
12. Administrator to Minister, 27 November 1972, PP.
13. P.N.G., HAD, vol. III, no. 11, p. 1376.

10

DEVOLUTION

The year 1972 saw the devolution of political power, though the effective assumption of that power lagged somewhat behind. At the end of the year I wrote:

> 1972 has been dominated by political and constitutional developments. . . . The devoted attention of the media to these aspects of national life has somewhat distorted perspectives and helped to create the impression that words are enough and that statements may be in lieu of action rather than a prelude to it. The component parts of the National Coalition Government, as yet, find difficulty in transplanting a somewhat nebulous political philosophy with policy decisions and executive action.[1]

We had devolved many powers and a *Government Gazette* of August 10 1972 formally listed the powers assumed by Papua New Guinea Ministers, but significant ones were still Australian responsibilities, the principal among them being the control of the Public Service, civil aviation, foreign trade, fisheries, broadcasting, central banking and currency, police, higher education, protective tariffs, justice and external revenue. All of these were to be transferred before 1 December 1973, while control of Foreign Affairs and Defence would not

pass over until independence. Australia was dis-
engaging but there was still a long way to go in the next
twelve months.

A second level of disengagement was less formal but
still important in the development of Papua New
Guinea self-confidence in its new government; that is,
the reduced posture of Australians within the Public
Service where they still headed up most of the Departments, and in particular that of the Administrator. My
first reduction in posture came soon after the election of
Michael Somare as Chief Minister when I terminated
the weekly press conferences which had been habitual
not only with me but also with my predecessor. This
meant that the press had to seek their news from the
Chief Minister whose press conference then took up
the slack left by the cessation of the Administrator's.
This ensured that news and the Chief Minister became
associated in the public eye. I then began a progressive
withdrawal from AEC deliberations. It should be noted
that within a few weeks the AEC was generally referred
to as the Cabinet, though in fact it combined the
functions performed in Executive Council and by
Cabinet in Australia. The *Papua New Guinea Act* set out
that the Administrator shall preside — a fiat which we
began to ignore as soon as the Chief Minister and his
Cabinet became familiar with their portfolios and
developed some procedures for dealing with business. I
began first by surrendering the Chair to the Chief
Minister when the topic of discussion lay within the
final power of a Minister of Papua New Guinea — a
transferred function — and when this was working
satisfactorily I withdrew from presiding altogether.
Next I withdrew from the meeting completely when
transferred functions were being dealt with, and attended only when the matters being discussed were still
Australian responsibilities. It should be noted that the

Australian Government made a practice of taking no decisions without reference to the Papua New Guinea Government, irrespective of whether it was a retained function or not. I cannot recall any occasion when it acted without Papua New Guinea concurrence.

Of the retained powers, those attracting most attention were those over police and defence. Though the latter was, with foreign affairs, over the horizon, Papua New Guineans were anxious to be involved in decisions as to its role. They were proud of this efficient force but alarmed at its cost, presently borne by the Australian Government, should that burden be thrust upon them, and also critical of the limited role it could play if confined to that dictated by Australian policy. Equipment, uniforms, barracks and general living standards made the police the poor relations but it was the police who bore the total burden not only of routine police duties in towns and villages but also the difficult and dangerous tasks of confronting and controlling mass disturbances such as those fomented by the Mataungans in the Gazelle Peninsula, and of intervening in tribal warfare in the highlands. The Pacific Islands Regiment (PIR) seemed to be principally engaged in war games, parades and training. Thus there was early pressure to have Ministers who would answer in the House of Assembly for the police and for defence and speak for the Papua New Guinea Government in related matters.

In a meeting in August 1972 the Minister for External Territories agreed to the creation of a spokesman for police and a similar position for defence. Somare, who assumed both posts, outlined the functions of the Defence Spokesman to:

(a) answer parliamentary questions and make statements on defence matters.
(b) consult the Administrator, present submissions to the AEC, and lead discussion in the AEC in regard

to the development of the Papua New Guinea forces and defence policies.

(c)   undertake ceremonial duties.[2]

The duties of the Police Spokesman were similar. We were particularly anxious that the PIR should begin to look to its own government and it was a theme I had earlier dwelt on myself in addressing 2 PIR in Wewak:

Army, people, Government are one thing and must work together. They are all citizens of Papua New Guinea and they all have the same rights and the same duties. And this is an important message we must all learn. People, army, Government are one. . . .

A Government can and should expect absolute loyalty from its people if that Government is of the people itself, if it is your government, if it is a Government which the people vote for freely, and if it is a government which can be criticized openly and freely, and if it is a government which you yourselves can form, can change by voting. . . .

The most important thing that people can expect of its Army is the absolute loyalty of the Army. The most important thing a people, and its Army, can expect from their government is the right to be able to change it if it isn't governing the country as they wish; and if these two things are maintained, if these two things are complementary, then we have the makings of a firm and stable government in Papua New Guinea and an army which can perform its role effectively and loyally to a government.[3]

Events in other developing countries had given rise to some unfounded fears that an independent government might, at some future time, be faced with an Army coup, for it was something of an alien growth in Papua New Guinea, and there had been some encouragement, in army circles, for the idea that the army itself was akin to a tribal group with its loyalties directed inward. At this time, 1972, almost all of its senior officers were white, though two Papua New Guineans had reached the rank of major. All officer training was carried out in Australia and a considerable proportion of other ranks had also had specialized training in Australia. The PIR was, in effect, a specialized arm of the Australian Defence Force.

Police matters were much closer to home for members of the House of Assembly. There was a police presence in every town and in many villages. Police accompanied patrols, police arrested malefactors, they intervened in tribal wars, they restrained the violent and rescued the injured; they were ubiquitous, and they were the presence representing the power of the government. Members did their best to look after the police in their electorates, and one of the common topics brought up at Question Time was the deficiencies in police accommodation. Yakob Talis had these comments to make:

(1) Is it a fact that the quarters of married police at Lumi and Nuku are in a deplorable condition?
(2) Is it also a fact that these quarters lack furniture and kitchen and washing facilities?
(3) Will he send an officer to investigate these conditions?
(4) If not, why not?[4]

It was very probably true and made for glaring comparisons between conditions for the police as against those enjoyed by the PIR.

There was yet another para-military force in Papua New Guinea — the prison warders — and it was this group which attracted John Guise to seek the Ministry of the Interior in preference to other more important and prestigious portfolios (I had endeavoured to persuade him to take Education). It was a devolved power and Guise was thus the only Minister to have a disciplined armed body under his command.

Control of foreign affairs was not scheduled to pass

to Papua New Guinea until independence but there were many matters which required the joint considera-tion of the two governments prior to that date. The most important of these were the border issues — P.N.G./Indonesia and P.N.G./Australia. The border with Indonesia was a matter requiring the utmost delicacy in handling, particularly because of the move-ment of refugees into Papua New Guinea to the north near Wutung and for the refuge dissidents sought on the Papua New Guinea side when Indonesian pressure forced precipitate retreat. The border with Australia was perhaps not of critical moment but it was certainly vexatious. All of the Torres Straits islands were Australian Territory, some of them within a kilometre or two of the Papuan coast. There was a constant passage to and from Torres Straits islands and the Western District of Papua. There were many kinship ties and some Papuans found it an easy passage to illegal residence in Australia, and, in due course, to the benefits of Australian social services. The Member for South Fly in the Western District was Ebia Olewale, Minister for Education, who had practically made a career out of complaints of the intruding Australian suzerainty. Olewale fired the first shot in a long cam-paign in 1969 in moving in the House of Assembly:

> That this House considers that the present state of the boundary between Papua and New Guinea and the State of Queensland which, in part, runs within 1.5 miles [2.4 km] of the coast of the Western District and includes a number of islands and reefs within a few miles of that coast and separated from Queensland by the whole width of the Torres Straits, is in all respects most unsatisfactory as time goes by, both because of the fact that the customary fishing grounds and reef of many Papuans as well as other natural resources that ought to belong to Papua and New Guinea and not situated in Queensland waters.[5]

In reaching an accommodation the Commonwealth Government was restricted because of the necessity to achieve a solution agreeable to the Queensland Government and the fact that the Torres Straits islanders had a very marked preference for remaining under the Australian flag.

Although independence and the consequent transfer of power over foreign relations to Papua New Guinea still seemed to be some years away, it was necessary to set up the framework, both in establishing a central office to consider such matters, and in training some officers for a diplomatic role. As early as 1971, we had set this in train and by 1972 we had a Foreign Affairs cell within the Department of the Administrator (shortly to become the Department of the Chief Minister). At the same time a Defence cell was established.[6] Some young Papua New Guinean officers who had completed a training course were attached to some of the Australian overseas posts for experience — initially to Djakarta and Bangkok.

At the end of 1972 I commented to the Minister for External Territories that:

> 1972 was the year in which foreign nations discovered Papua New Guinea. The increased publicity consequent on rapid constitutional advance and on the commencement of production of the Bougainville copper mine were in part responsible for increased foreign interest. Not unexpectedly the Japanese led the way with their interest firmly based on large loans to the copper mining company and to a number of earlier appraisals by teams of experts. The year saw the beginning of a Japanese timber chipping industry in Madang, the negotiation of joint venture tuna fishing agreements with Japanese companies and the finalizing of agreement to a Japanese-financed oil palm project in New Britain. Mitsui opened an office in Port Moresby and a Japanese company bought out Placer Development's interests in P.N.G. The participation of P.N.G.

Ministers in the Australia/Japanese Ministerial talks signalled our coming independent status and our disposition to look for aid from countries additional to Australia, and in particular, from those whose economic interests benefited from infrastructure already established.

Other countries were slower off the mark except that Indonesia, more anxious about our common border, was the first country to seek consular representation in Port Moresby. Nevertheless there was a growing number of visitors from other countries: U.S.A., Canada, the U.K., France, New Zealand, Yugoslavia, South Korea, all came prospecting for opportunities.

Papua New Guinea's ties with the Pacific countries were strengthened somewhat by its conditional admission to the South Pacific Forum and by the emotions aroused by the French atomic tests, but there was a general consensus that the dominant continuing influences on Papua New Guinea would be Australia, Indonesia and Japan.[7]

I have referred previously to the firm intention of Papua New Guineans to control their own air waves. We planned to supplant the ABC with a similar Papua New Guinea commission to be called the National Broadcasting Commission (NBC) which would control all broadcasting throughout the country. The Minister for Information, Paulus Arek, told the House "the view of my government is that broadcasting in Papua New Guinea, as in other developing countries, must be used to develop national unity and to foster other national goals. The authority would be required to provide as a public service an independent and impartial broadcasting service".[8] Independence and impartiality are unusual attributes in the broadcasting service of very many countries. The NBC saw the light of day in 1973 with a Tolai, Sam Piniau, as its first Chief. During my stay in Papua New Guinea I always thought that the ABC did not treat us too kindly in its news and information broadcasts. Sam Piniau and the NBC also found it difficult to satisfy the government of its impartiality.

I have also referred to the planning to set up Air Niugini which was formally born on 30 October 1973, but we had also established a small office to supplant, in due course, the Australian Department of Civil Aviation, which controlled all flying in Papua New Guinea and managed and serviced the major airports. It was a formidable task but most capably fulfilled by Bill Bradfield until we had an indigenous officer sufficiently experienced to take over.

The areas which had been Australian responsibilities, but outside the jurisdiction of the Papua New Guinea Administration, had been laggard in the indigenization process and had few Papua New Guineans within their ranks to assume responsible executive posts. These agencies were within the Australian Public Service, bound by its attitudes and its regulations, with Australian public servants rotating in Papua New Guinea for a two or three year term. They had neither direction nor incentive to provide executive training for Papua New Guineans. The Reserve Bank was a shining exception. In other cases the Papua New Guinean government had to rob its own Departments of scarce skills and experience to meet expanding demands.

If 1972 had been a year of devolution, 1973 was the year in which we had to put it all together.

NOTES

1. Administrator to Minister for External Territories, 21 December 1972, PP.
2. P.N.G., House of Assembly Debates (HAD), vol. III, no. 5, p. 462.
3. Address at Moem Barracks, 24 February 1971, PP.
4. P.N.G., HAD, vol. III, no. 11, p. 1307.
5. P.N.G., HAD, vol. II, no. 6, p. 1485.

6. Colin McDonald from Foreign Affairs and Nick Webb from Defence were Australian officers seconded to head up these cells as a preliminary establishment measure.
7. Administrator to Minister for External Territories, 21 December 1972, PP.
8. P.N.G., HAD, vol. III, no. 5, p. 423.

11

SOCIETY IN TRANSITION

Rural Papua New Guinea remained a country of discrete villages dependent on annual food crops for a living, supported by animal husbandry with pigs and some hunting and gathering. Pigs and cassowaries were normally consumed only on special occasions. Coastal villages were more fortunate than their inland brothers as stands of coconuts provided a firm base for their livelihood and a cash income as well. For the New Guinean the cultivation of tree crops other than coconuts for cash came later; first was cacao, initially in the Gazelle Peninsula, but spreading to other lowland areas, then coffee in the Highlands followed by tea, and other high altitude crops such as the pyrethrum daisy. In the late sixties cattle were introduced as a small-holder pastoral enterprise. I recall the anguish of some of our officers when occasionally an expensive breeding bull was butchered by the villagers for an important festival. Rubber, near the coast, was always a plantation crop until efforts in the sixties produced a number of small-holder growers.

Outwardly life in the villages seemed much the same. For those with cash there were some exotic commodities which could be purchased at the trade store —

still mostly expatriate-owned. Rice, canned fish and meat and beer were available, which meant less reliance on the traditional food crops. There were radios which told of the outside world, and there were visitors from other tribes and other countries to buy the crops now produced locally. In many villages there was a school which, for better or for worse, changed the aspirations of the young, and there was a movement of young men away from the tedium of village life where exciting ceremonies were now less frequent and where tribal wars were forbidden or at least their practice restrained. The biggest change of all, in part produced by cash cropping and the need for the hand of the government to reach further into the life of the people, was the arrival of the road. The road was the umbilical connection uniting the part with the whole. The future of the village was now inescapably linked with that of the developing nation.

Cash crops, schools and roads began the inevitable transformation of village society and with this was associated yet another fundamental change. At least until the early sixties the law, as dictated by the colonial power, was administered, largely, by its field officers. In rural areas they judged and they punished. The field officers commanded the police, set up the courts in which they were judge, advocate and jury, and they controlled the prison to which malefactors were sent. Justice — or at least punishment — was administered on the spot, and promptly. Though, no doubt, inexperienced young field officers were often hoodwinked by the villagers, everyone understood the rules. The "kiap" had power and, with it, prestige.

In the sixties the system was supplanted by what might be termed the "Australianization" of the administration of the law. Independent judges, magistrates and professional lawyers took the place of the kiaps and rules of evidence took the place of the free-wheeling methods of the past. Lawyers now argued points of law. Given that evidence was often produced by illiterate policemen and unsophisticated villagers, there were many occasions when an offender, who every villager knew was guilty, escaped the consequences of his act through some mysterious legality argued learnedly, in English, before a be-robed judge and a bemused audience. An old-time expatriate related an apocryphal story about the new courts with relish. A villager was being tried for murder and was asked by the judge how he pleaded. When the judge's words were translated into pidgin for him, he stood proudly proclaiming "Yesa mi amamas mi kilim i dai" (Yes I am pleased I killed him), whereupon his court-appointed counsel rose, saying "Your honour, my client pleads not guilty!" Anyway, the administration of the law became remote and intolerably slow. Sometimes many months elapsed before cases could be heard; the law came into disrepute, and there was a lessening regard for its observance.

The change in the administration of the law was only one factor in the growth of lawlessness in Papua New Guinea; society was being transformed and the process of adjustment was slow and painful. The mores of a village society were challenged by the young, the authority of the elders was being eroded but there was as yet nothing to take its place. For the Government it meant a number of acute problems and perhaps the first of these was the recrudescence of tribal warfare in the highlands.

As land was life, tribal conflict over land was endemic where there was little cultivable land and dense populations. As the government control extended over these areas the tribes were coerced to accept arbitration — by the man on the spot — and boundaries were established and frozen. But in the sixties the authority of the man on the spot diminished, respect for a remote government was reduced and talk of self-government induced aggrieved tribal groups to set out to recoup ancient losses before a new authority was in place.

In the past I had seen one white officer[1] intrude himself between two factions about to commence hostilities and stop the impending warfare. In the seventies we sometimes had as many as four police riot squads equipped with tear gas, some shotguns, batons and shields, trying to prevent a fight and failing. Warriors came to battle equipped with bows, arrows, axes, clubs and a jute bag, the last named to smother the tear gas canisters.

Deaths were not numerous in these affrays, sometimes perhaps one or two killed and a considerable number wounded but a death of a man from one group inevitably meant that the other side was obligated to even the score — if not immediately, then at some other more propitious occasion, though sometimes it was possible to short-circuit a pay-back killing by arranging a compensation payment in cash and in kind. But apart from this, widespread damage was caused. Houses were burned and crops uprooted, the object being to do as much material damage to the enemy as possible.

The road brought us problems, too. The road, as far as most Papua New Guineans were concerned, was the road from Lae into the highlands. It was begun by an energetic District Commissioner in Goroka, Ian Downs, who enlisted the labour of tribesmen to cut a track to the coast. In the sixties it was gradually upgraded, and an all-weather road (mostly) climbed up the mountains from the coastal plain, reached Goroka and extended to Mount Hagen in the Western Highlands. In the seventies it reached Mendi in the Southern Highlands. It was the road which revolutionized highlands transport. Previously all freight, in and out of the highlands, was carried by air, at great cost. The road made trucking possible and reduced costs greatly. But it also made for very many accidents caused by inexperienced drivers, poor road conditions and the like, and for every death there was a demand, from fellow tribesmen of the deceased, for exhorbitant compensation payments, or a "pay-back" killing was planned. Sometimes enraged villagers killed the driver of the offending vehicle on the spot.

Truck travel through the highlands also introduced a socio-medical problem with the spread of venereal disease through a community highly vulnerable to introduced infections. One of the agencies was the proliferation of part-time prostitution by young village women who became known as "passenger meris". They would sit by the roadside blatantly displaying their wares until picked up by a truck and transported along the highway, and returned home in a similar way. It was necessary to introduce crash V.D. control measures to check what might have become a serious medical problem.

The passage of trucks laden with goods also tempted the bold. On the long slow climb up the mountain trucks were vulnerable to individuals who would jump on the back undetected and throw off whatever they could reach to accomplices on the roadside. It became necessary to have someone riding "shotgun" on the back, some of whom were not averse to a bit of collusion with roadside gangs.

The growth of towns presented a different set of social problems and these were particularly apparent in Port Moresby, whose enumerated population was growing at ten per cent annually plus a considerable percentage who evaded enumeration and could only be guessed at. Both burglary and violent attacks on individuals increased dramatically and it would be easy to blame it all on the footloose young men who migrated to the city lights. Certainly, they may have been responsible for much personal violence, both within their own groups and in bar-room brawls between antagonistic groups but there was also an alarming increase in organized crime by gangs of youths whose permanent homes were in and around the city. They were commonly referred to as "the rascals" and as their capacity to evade capture and retribution increased, so their boldness grew commensurately. The under-manned under-equipped and under-trained police did their best but it was not enough to contain the increase in lawlessness.

Port Moresby was an urban melting pot. The original inhabitants were far outnumbered by the new arrivals. At the base of the urban pile were the original villagers concentrated in or near the city, the largest group in Hanuabada village, a stone's throw from Government House. Then there were successive slices of migrants forming separate groups in the community but cautiously coalescing on the fringes. The latest arrivals were footloose young men, mostly from the highlands. They soon found that the streets were not paved with gold and by and large they were the unemployed proletariat of the town, restless, sometimes hungry and often violent. It was an explosive mixture that erupted into a wild riot on 22 and 23 July in 1973, when the annual Papua versus New Guinea rugby match was played. Football matches are often the cause for riotous behaviour in many countries and we always took precautions for these gladiatorial contests in Papua New Guinea but the violence of this one took us by surprise. It began in the football ground when highlanders (New

Guinea supporters) attacked Papuan spectators, but it rapidly spilled over the fence into the surrounding suburbs and beyond, and soon became general. It lasted for two days and two nights. The football match provided the spark which caused the explosion, but the causes were much more deep-seated. At the time I set out to try to explain it:

The causes of the riots which broke out after a football match on Sunday 22 July have been analyzed by many experts and many somewhat less than experts. For my part I would regard the Port Moresby situation in the sixties and seventies as fruitful ground for riots irrespective of extraneous circumstances. Riots of significance have occurred on a number of occasions. The root causes are the rapid growth of the town and in particular the influx of young men looking for change, excitement, work, escape from the tedium of village life. Most of these migrants are uneducated and unskilled. In very many cases they have no work and depend upon fellow tribesmen for food and shelter. They are a seed bed for all possible variation of trouble — bar room brawls when they have money for drink, housebreakings, assaults upon women, tribal confrontations and riots, self-induced and otherwise. In an earlier period these migrants came from adjacent coastal areas and had a common language with the regional Port Moresby inhabitants and some similarity in cultural background. Even so they were, and sometimes still are, a source of trouble and of tribal or regional brawls. The people from the Gulf District still figure prominently in many Port Moresby disturbances. However, jobs, importation of wives and the production of families, houses, even if in shanty town conditions, were a stablizing influence and the Gulf people have become acceptable and permanent Port Moresby citizens. Another influx in later years was from the Goilala area only a few days' walk from Port Moresby. One always assumed that a large-scale brawl would have Goilalas as a contending party. They are now beginning to bring their women into town and assuming virtuous critical attitudes towards the latest invasion wave from the highlands.

The latest influx is somewhat different from the earlier ones in that it is greater in numbers and thus very much more obvious. The migrants come from a culture which in some respects is significantly different from that of the established inhabitants of the town and furthermore they have little or no prospect of returning home should they wish to do so because of the cost of an air fare (Port Moresby — Kundiawa $28-10 single).

Thus in 1973 there was a large group of men from various Highlands Districts in Port Moresby with little chance of association with women, even prostitutes, frustrated by failing to find the Eldorado they sought, free from the inhibitions associated with family and clan obligations, bored, envious of the established inhabitants and ripe for any sort of mischief providing relief and release.

Political talk, parliamentarians' posturing and regional rivalries coalesced at this time into an issue of such simplicity that all could understand — that is, the cry of Papua for the Papuans. The Papua Besena Movement led by Miss Abaijah is not new. It has been a recurrent theme since substantial development funds began to flow to Papua New Guinea, mostly to the more immediately productive areas in New Guinea or into the town of Port Moresby. Western District, Gulf, Milne Bay and Central Districts, other than Port Moresby, saw little of the money. Papua, an Australian colony, Papuan Australian citizens saw themselves as something special whose particular relationship with Australia was being overlooked. In the early years these feelings were channelled into the Seventh State idea — the incorporation initially of the whole of Papua New Guinea into Australia but failing that, the union of all Australian citizens excluding the New Guineas. Australians with investments in Papua actively promoted this movement which appeared to die finally and conclusively in 1967 when the Minister for External Territories firmly killed it. It was resurrected in a new form a few years later, this time inspired by Papuan politicians planning for a greater share of development funds. Australian citizenship rights and Australia's special responsibility for Papua were the principal arguments used in promoting the movement. The first of these was catered for by hiring a consultant group to report on assistance to under-developed areas in Papua New Guinea and later uniform development became an accepted aim of the Papua New Guinea Government. The last two contentions were firmly squashed by an authorized statement from the Administrator in 1971.

The Papua Besena Movement is yet another attempt to claim a special Australia-Papua relationship. It presses for a greater share of the development cake and adds a new element in calling for deportation of large numbers of New Guineans (highlanders by inference) and strict control of the migration of new ones. The wide publicity given to Miss Abijah's statements, and the anti-New Guinea stance of her followers, produced an obvious reaction and lowered the riot flashpoint dangerously. Although a football match provided the spark it could well have been any other incident.

It is interesting to note that, apart from the preliminary in-ground brawl, the initial actions of the rioters were not specifically directed against Papuans; rather was it a communal release of the tensions of urban living, a sort of mindless vandalism directed at the ranks of privilege, those with families, cars, houses and the other appurtenances of affluence. Only later did Papuans as a group become the target for violence and even then in an impersonal sort of way by the throwing of missiles at cars and houses.

On the following day the various tribal groups gathered, initially for mutual protection, but with highlanders still the aggressors. The nature of the groupings ensured that sporadic encounters between these groups were essentially tribal, or better, regional conflicts. However, the immediate pressures had been released and the social temperature was quickly lowered, although rumour remained rife. It seems likely that similar disturbances may occur given that the general urban situation is unlikely to change significantly and that contentious incidents are bound to occur from time to time.[2]

As the riot subsided the AEC met to consider what preventive measures were possible. Suggestions ranged over a wide area, from the Chief Minister's proposal that rioters should be shot, to the wholesale deportation of all highlanders, this latter suggestion made in the absence of highland Ministers who had been unable to get to a meeting called at such short notice. Ultimately it was agreed that measures to control migration to the towns be submitted for future Council consideration and that I should be authorized to declare that the section of the Public Order Ordinance providing for control of processions and meetings be brought into force in Port Moresby town.

Migration to the towns of unskilled young men continued to be a problem and from time to time the introduction of "pass laws" was considered, but the South African example was hardly one to emulate and no action was taken to control the unfettered movement of the country's citizens.

The advent of a genuine home grown government was also a spur to revive interest in Papua New Guinea culture. The Chief Minister himself, coming from the artistically productive Sepik river, and the son of a skilful wood carver, was anxious to promote indigenous cultural activity and found many, both black and white, who were eager to support him. Particularly active and successful was the Director of Education, Ken McKinnon, whose interest ensured that schools became centres of original artistic activity. Everywhere almost forgotten arts were revived and married with modern ideas and materials, producing a rich harvest of painting, sculpture, dance, drama and literature. A Cultural Centre was established where creative people from all over the country were brought for periods of residence to practise their arts and pass on their skills. The first novel by a Papua New Guinean had been published earlier, in 1970; this was *The Crocodile* by Vincent Eri,[3] a good friend of mine, who sent my wife and me a copy inscribed "I'm not sure whether this is a slur or an honour to the expatriates; there's nothing in it that you do not already know about yourselves." Novelists, poets, short story writers and playwrights proliferated, many writing in the vernacular languages of their home villages or in Pidgin.

Much of the new writing came from the University and perhaps inevitably it was anti-establishment and anti-white. But possibly the greatest change in Papua New Guinea society was the changed nature of race relations in the country, for the pupils and servants of past years had now become the masters. Papua New Guineans now had patronage to dispense. Some whites welcomed the change with enthusiasm, in particular, university staff who provided much of the technical advice that Papua New Guinean Ministers were hesitant to receive from the Public Service. Some, particularly the well established planter and business-man community, who had unthinkingly accepted a privileged status as their birthright, found it hard to adjust to a society in which, though they might be tolerated, they were no longer privileged. Public servants on the whole adjusted pretty well, once a satisfactory employment security scheme was approved, and did their best to help the new Government succeed. Social functions of a public nature became thoroughly and companionably mixed, though white and black tended to remain within their own circles in private affairs. There had always been a good many marriages between expatriate men and Papua New Guinean women but rarely had an expatriate woman married a Papua New Guinean man — for instance the marriage of John Kaputin to an Australian teacher in 1961 had been highly controversial. Now, though still not common, such marriages were not considered remarkable events. My wife and I got many sour looks from expatriates as our guest lists for official functions contained smaller and smaller proportions of whites as Papua New Guineans assumed more of the positions of importance in the community.

The question left for the future to answer was "Is a black elite taking the place of a white one?" Such was certainly not the intention of the government. I tried to set out its objectives in a despatch to the Minister for External Territories in December 1972.

> But policy formulation in respect of the elements that go to make up a nation is only a means to an attempt to determine what sort of a Papua New Guinean society one should strive to achieve. Our Government [the Papua New Guinea Government], believes that, at this stage of the country's development, it is possible to determine what sort of society is most desirable and to take action to create an environment in which it can develop. Although the miasma of Australian hedonism overlies the educated Papua New Guineans there is plenty of debate about creating something that is different. The ideal Papua New Guinean should live a simple unostentatious life, hold fast to the traditions of his people, achieve respect and status by his personal qualities and share his possessions. Although many societies would subscribe to such an ideal, Papua New Guineans feel that they have not yet departed so far from simple rural values that a whole society cannot be created here, in actuality, in this image. The Government aspires to a nation when the basic necessities of life are available to all in sufficient quantity and quality, where all may be educated, where government services are provided for all, adequately and equally, and where no man is rich, and none is a beggar.[4]

It is now ten years later but Papua New Guinea does not seem to be too much closer to this Utopia and the life-style of many politicians seems to indicate that they no longer subscribe to this ideal.

NOTES

1. It was Mick Foley, then District Commissioner in the Chimbu, since deceased.
2. Memorandum, 1 August 1973, PP.
3. Eri is presently Head of the Department of Defence.
4. Administrator to Minister for External Territories, 21 December 1972, PP.

12

THE ECONOMY
(NOT IN TRANSITION)

Government aspirations for the sort of society set out in the previous chapter required an economic framework for its realization. I continued to try to outline how the government hoped to do it.

There is a recognition that such a society is not attainable within an unfettered, free enterprise system, and there is a groping for a means to exploit private capital and modern technology for the benefit of all, through State controls and State participation. At present we lack capacity to undertake the social and economic engineering necessary to make a total transformation, but the Government is determined to take what steps it may to bring it about. The practical measures are likely to be an attempt to set more rigid guidelines than at present on foreign investment proposals, to increase substantially development grants to rural areas, probably through Area Authorities, to adjust taxation rates on both individuals and companies; to seek to do much more to equalize living standards. there will be the most careful scouting of major projects to ensure adequate benefits for Papua New Guinea and its indigenous inhabitants. High quality and high cost infrastructure, such as road building financed by international borrowings, may be replaced by smaller scale projects using local labour and local materials. . . . The total picture is of an overall equaliz-

ing of expenditure distribution and of services and
facilities which would mean a considerable reduction in
existing standards in towns.[1]

The first rather modest step in this direction did not
come until August 1973 with the doubling of the allocation to rural development funds — grants to local
government councils for small scale projects within
their areas of responsibility.

In overall terms Papua New Guinea's economy in
1972, the first year of office for the new Government,
was in recession; 1972, in some respects, was a year of
problems, even of disasters. There was a localized
cyclonic disturbance which devastated large areas surrounding the town of Tufi in the Northern District, and
drought afflicted almost the whole of Papua New
Guinea, sharply reducing yields of both subsistence and
cash crops. Associated with the drought came a succession of very severe frosts which created a famine crisis
for 140,000 people in the highlands. Quite apart from
natural disasters the price of the principal export commodities remained very low on world markets and
Papua New Guinea's terms of trade deteriorated. Copra
was at its lowest price level since 1948, rubber was
severely depressed, while, within the circumscribing
arms of the International Coffee Agreement, Papua
New Guinea had disposal problems for a considerable
proportion of its coffee crop.

Of other forms of economic activity dependent on
outside interest and capital, the one most markedly
affected was mineral prospecting which had assumed
the proportions of a major industry. Although there
was a marked decline in mineral exploration, it was not
entirely due to a little sabre rattling by some P.N.G.
Ministers and others, but also to a world-wide
downturn in prospecting, as metals production over-
took and surpassed demand. However, it was true that

some major companies curtailed their activities in Papua New Guinea pending clarification of the government's policy towards mining ventures.

In other respects it was evident that there was a substantially greater participation by Papua New Guineans in the cash economy and a significant increase in entrepreneurial activities by local businessmen financed by Development Bank loans, Savings and Loan Societies, and other sources of credit not subject to the rigidities imposed by the Australian-based trading banks. Construction contracting by Papua New Guineans developed well, though mostly they worked as subcontractors rather than principals. On the rural front there was a big increase in the numbers of cattle pastured by Papua New Guinean farmers.

Of course an economy dependent largely on tropical tree crops was always at risk because the producers of these commodities were the poorer countries of the world with little bargaining muscle when dealing with the great and powerful nations which provided their main markets. Prices fluctuated widely and the peasant producer might be reasonably affluent in one season and find, in the next year, that his income might be halved. Stabilization funds, producers' and consumers' joint efforts to regulate the markets, could, and did, even out the extreme fluctuations, but it was always difficult to explain to the individual grower that his government had little influence on prices paid on a world market.

In the early seventies the principal sources of export income came from copra, cocoa and coffee with smaller supplements from rubber and tea. Timber was produced and sold and a new tree crop, palm oil, began producing and showed promise. We looked forward to diversification and a considerable increase in export income, and in Government revenue, with the Bougainville copper mine coming on stream. We were trying, without too much success, to expand a fishing industry. There were also a number of expatriate-owned cattle runs and we had begun to encourage small-holders to keep and breed cattle. In Port Moresby and Lae small scale industry providing for local needs had been established but the great bulk of our requirements were still imported, mostly from Australia. For 1971–72 Papua New Guinea exports were valued at $93.5 million, and that included $23 million from the copper mine, while imports were worth $228.3 million. For the 1972–73 financial year the Papua New Guinea government budgeted for an expenditure of $222.65 million, of which only $95 million could be provided from internal sources. The gap was filled by overseas borrowing and by an Australian grant of $78.5 million, plus an additional $42.8 million for overseas officers' allowances.[2] Such dependence on Australia was not the best of all possible beginnings for a new Papua New Guinea government; it certainly set limits on its future independence of action, given that the gap between income and expenditure would be impossible to bridge unless some extraordinary bonanzas turned up.

There were some possibilities over the horizon — principally in the discovery of two further significant copper occurrences on the main island, one on each side of the dividing cordillera close to the border with Irian Jaya — one, Ok Tedi, in the mountainous hinterland of the Western District and the other across the divide in the Sepik District. They were both remote and inhospitable sites in which to establish mines, but the Ok Tedi prospect looked particularly promising as the cap of the deposit contained a significant percentage of gold. Ok Tedi was hope continuously deferred; only in 1981 did major companies accept the feasibility of profitable development.

There was also hope that oil might be found in marketable quantities. There had been sporadic exploration for oil in Papua from the beginning of the century with occasional oil shows, and more frequent gas flows, to sustain hope but commercial discoveries eluded the searchers. Papua New Guinea did, however, have greater resources of water power and a great deal of trouble was taken to interest big overseas companies in the vast hydro-electric potential provided by the Purari River as it plunged from the central mountains on to the plain. Expertise and capital were needed for a major export fishing industry, in particular to exploit the elusive streams of tuna that patrol the Pacific.

It was at this time that Japan, or at least individual Japanese companies, began to take an interest in Papua New Guinea. It was an interest initially generated by the visits of groups of Japanese war veterans coming to the old battlefields and burial grounds to recover the bones of the dead and take them home. Then came individuals looking for a fast yen, and interested principally in exporting timber in logs, whereas we wanted industries that would process the timber in Papua New Guinea. They were followed by companies interested, but cautious, though pretty soon every affluent Papua New Guinean seemed to have a Toyota truck or utility.

We were cautious too. We recognized that Papua New Guinea could not be insulated but we doubted the skill and experience of the Papua New Guinea Government to cope with the Japanese. As early as 1971 the Department of External Territories had reviewed the Japanese-Papua New Guinea relationship and come to the conclusion that "it is clear that increased access to Japan's market will be crucial to the Territory's trading problems in the foreseeable future."[3] The Australian Embassy in Japan commented, "We would rate the Japanese economic interest in the Territory as, at the

moment, marginally more important than that of war-
time associations or tourism, and almost certain to
become the major interest in the future. Basically this
economic interest is simply that of obtaining access to
needed raw materials."[4]

The new Papua New Guinea Government was a bit
more bullish about relations with Japan than was its
mentor, Australia. Somare can still sing a lullaby in
Japanese taught to him by Japanese soldiers in Wewak
during World War II. He had visited Japan in 1971 and
been well received; Japanese who were involved in
business ventures in Papua New Guinea had behaved
with the utmost circumspection and in general the
Ministers of Papua New Guinea did not see Japanese investors or Japanese ventures as endangering their
economic and social goals any more than similar activities by Australians did. It was a point of view that
Australians were curiously reluctant to accept.
However representatives of the Papua New Guinea
Government were invited to participate in the deliberations of the Japan/Australia Ministerial Committee in
October 1972. For the new Ministers, it was a
prestigious occasion, the first time they had been formally recognized internationally. Somare addressed
himself to the economic relationship.

> I believe that the Japanese market will become in-
> creasingly important for Papua New Guinea in the
> future and I hope to see increasing quantities of Papua
> New Guinean goods finding markets there. . . . I would
> like to add that Papua New Guinea has a non-
> discriminating tariff.[5] . . . as a consequence Papua New
> Guinea notes with appreciation efforts by countries
> such as Japan and Australia . . . to achieve progressive
> reduction of barriers to agricultural trade. . . . Regard-
> ing investment, Papua New Guinea is pleased to see a
> number of Japanese ventures successfully undertaken in
> Papua New Guinea and others under negotiation.

Papua New Guinea welcomes investment from Japanese companies which will
- assist in developing the country on a sound and balanced basis;
- provide opportunities for significant local equity; . . .
- make provision for employment and training opportunities for local people;
- involve maximum processing of products in Papua New Guinea;
- involve the enterprise in the provision of maximum common user facilities (e.g. roads, ports, etc.); . . .
Ultimately decisions on investment projects . . . are based on whether proposals fit into the pattern and shape of social and political development of the country. Particular emphasis is of course placed on opportunities for Papua New Guinea people to participate in the ownership and management of projects. Papua New Guinea, like most countries, is anxious to avoid excessive control of its resources by foreign countries and embraces the joint venture concept of development.[6]

Ohira, then the Japanese Foreign Minister, responded carefully:

I would like to assure you that in having economic and technological activities in the area concerned we would try to accommodate the real situation and the wishes of the country and contribute to the economic development and social stability of Papua New Guinea. In other words we have no specific ambition to go into the area but we would like to put first and foremost emphasis on the needs, desires and wishes of Papua New Guinea.
but
We would like to respect the position of Australia from that point of view, and to match our activities with the wishes and desires of the Australian Government in extending our economic and technological assistance to Papua New Guinea.[7]

Somare accepted an invitation to visit Japan in 1973 but Papua New Guinea's hopes for substantial aid from

Japan were not realized, offers of assistance being confined to minor amounts of technological assistance. Nor was there a headlong rush of Japanese investors nor any significant increase in Papua New Guinea's exports to Japan, except of course for the contractual arrangement between Bougainville Copper and Japanese interests which provided for the export of 1.1 million tonnes of contained copper over fifteen years, commencing in 1972. There was, however, a very considerable increase in Japanese exports to Papua New Guinea, stimulated by the large Japanese trading houses setting up branches in Port Moresby. Such Japanese investment as did occur was marginal to the economy of Papua New Guinea.

The principal interest of the Japanese, other than in the copper produced in Bougainville, lay in ensuring participation in exploiting tuna fishing in Papua New Guinea waters, with an eye on the possibility of control by Papua New Guinea of a vastly expanded area of surrounding sea which might arise out of the law of the sea negotiations. There was some interest also in Papua New Guinea's timber resources, but rather as a future source of supply when areas closer to home had been exhausted. The only area in which the Japanese presence became more and more obvious was in the consumer goods appearing in the shops and in Japanese dominance of the motor vehicle market. As it turned out Japan was not a threat to industry in Papua New Guinea, but it did indeed seize a share of what had been a captive Australian market. Neither did Japan provide much impetus to the Papua New Guinea economy, nor was Japan's aid of any consequence. All in all, the Japanese relationship was a bit of a disappointment to the Papua New Guinea Government.

Port Moresby was a long way from Europe and most Papua New Guineans neither knew of, or cared about, events there. But those responsible for selling Papua

New Guinea's exports on the international market were increasingly concerned that the country would be frozen out of traditional markets in the United Kingdom and Germany by common action within the European Economic Community (EEC). We were anxious to retain our preferred status but concerned that the trading privileges extended to previous colonies of the EEC countries would freeze us out. We put up the rather specious argument that as a colony of a previous British colony, and bearing in mind that Papua had been a British colony, we were entitled to the same status as, say, Fiji or Senegal, and in 1971 we despatched a mission to knock on European doors to plead our case. It was led by Angmai Bilas, the Ministerial Member for Trade and Industry, and supported by a team of experts who got a good hearing in most places (France was the exception), and ultimately Papua New Guinea was admitted to the favoured ranks of ex-colonies, the Lomē Convention, thus saving, in particular, our United Kingdom market for copra.

All this rather laboured description brings me to the concluding point — there had been no fundamental changes in the Papua New Guinea economy in the first two years of office of the Somare government, though that government had professed general objectives which might make for significant changes in the future. There had been no expropriation of property or of business. Expatriates were still making good profits and drawing good salaries. The capitalist framework was still firmly in place and the large companies were not under threat. The small individual expatriate entrepeneur was certainly insecure; he would be, or was being, replaced by black entrepeneurs, just as eager to exploit their brothers for profit. Transformation to Papua New Guinea ownership and Papua New Guinea management was going to be a lengthy process and it

seemed unlikely that the socialist millennium promised
by some politicians was very close at hand.

NOTES

1. Administrator to Minister for External Territories, 21 December 1972,
   PP.
2. Figures from P.N.G., House of Assembly Debates (HAD), vol. III, no.
   5, p. 438 — presentation of annual Appropriation Bill.
3. "Papua New Guinea and Japan", Department for External Territories,
   1971, PP.
4. Ibid.
5. Required under the UN Trusteeship Agreement.
6. Statement by the Chief Minister to the Australia/Japan Ministerial
   Committee, 13 October 1972, PP.
7. Statement of Foreign Minister of Japan to the Australia/Japan
   Ministerial Committe, 13 October 1972, PP.

13

LABOR AND PAPUA NEW GUINEA

The end of 1972 also saw the end of the McMahon coalition government in Australia. Gough Whitlam became Prime Minister and Bill Morrison the Minister for External Territories. The National Coalition Government (NCG) in Papua New Guinea welcomed the change, for it regarded Whitlam as its godfather, but it was less anxious to embrace publicly Whitlam's statement that independence could be obtained inside two years. Somare was quick to emphasize that decisions on his country's future would be made by the people of Papua New Guinea. At his weekly press conference on 7 December 1972 he mentioned this:

> I said before the elections that the result would not affect us much in any way at all whether we have to deal with a Liberal or Australian Labor Party Government. . . . I'd like to make this quite clear that I believe any independence date should be set by the people of this country and that the date would have to be endorsed by the House of Assembly. Now it's not a decision that should be made by anyone else.[1]

In other respects the Papua New Guineans were sorry to see Peacock disappear from the scene. He had established excellent relations with Somare and had made it clear that he was content for Papua New Guinea to call the shots. His successor, Morrison, had a difficult task. Like all new Ministers, he wanted to get his teeth into his portfolio and make an impact on events, whereas all of the key decisions had been made previously. The self-government date was fixed, a timetable for the transfer of functions was in place and being followed and NCG Ministers were resentful of pressure to do what they fully intended to do in any case. There were, however, a number of loose ends to be tied up and an early meeting between the principals of the two Governments was needed. So, shortly after the Australian Labor Government took office, Papua New Guinea let it be known that it was keen for the Chief Minister to meet Prime Minister Whitlam.

Quite apart from the need for some personal understanding to be developed, there was early uncertainty as to whether or not Papua New Guinea affairs would be the responsibility of the Department of Foreign Affairs, of which the Prime Minister was also the Minister. Also, the Prime Minister's visits to Papua New Guinea in 1969–70 and in 1971 when he was Leader of the Opposition might well be claimed to have been responsible for the accelerated pace of political development in Papua New Guinea, and in particular for the transfer of final powers to Papua New Guinea Ministers in July 1970 by the then Prime Minister, John Gorton. There was also a general expectation that a few promises as to future aid might be extracted from the Prime Minister before the Commonwealth Treasury had had time to indoctrinate its new masters.

Ultimately the meeting was fixed for 17 January 1973 and as a curtain raiser, or a mini-summit, the new Minister for External Territories visited Papua New Guinea and flew through to Wewak on 4 January for preliminary discussions with the Chief Minister on 5

January. I accompanied him. Between them, Somare and Morrison defined the matters to be discussed with the Prime Minister as follows:

- Date of self-government and independence
- Papua New Guinea/Queensland border
- Australian aid to Papua New Guinea and in particular the possibility of the Australian grant being guaranteed over a triennium
- Australian attitude towards aid for Papua New Guinea from Japan
- Fishing licences for Papua New Guinea ships in the Gulf of Carpentaria

Attitudes were canvassed at the Wewak meeting and it became apparent that there were unlikely to be serious differences of opinion at the Canberra meeting. Of particular interest was the Minister for External Territories' conviction that Australia would make a triennial commitment to the aid programme. This was something for which previously we had striven in vain.

Of direct and personal interest to both parties was agreement on a date for independence. Both Somare and Morrison were "sooner rather than later" men but Somare's problems with his coalition partner, the People's Progress Party, and the likely unfavourable public reaction in the highlands to an early independence date made him cautious about public commitments. Morrison and Somare agreed that a suitable date for independence would be National Day (September 15) 1974 but also agreed that this was a private commitment and not for public revelation. Somare implied that he would be happy for it to be seen that Australian pressure was forcing an early date for independence. Morrison, perhaps misunderstanding the politics of independence in Papua New Guinea, then embarrassed Somare at a press conference by referring to independence during 1974. Somare had no option but to hedge and qualify the date.

Preparations for the Canberra meeting proceeded and very adequate briefing papers were put together for all parties — the Chief Minister, the Minister for External Territories and the Australian Prime Minister. A draft communique was prepared on the assumption that there was unlikely to be any contention on the major topics to be discussed.

I went to Canberra for a meeting with the Minister for External Territories on 16 January to ensure that the approaching summit would be free of discord. Prior to the meeting on 17 January the Minister for External Territories, the Secretary, External Territories and I further briefed the Prime Minister.

The stage was also set in other directions by the Prime Minister despatching an aircraft of the VIP Flight to Brisbane to pick up the Chief Minister and party and bring them to Canberra, and both the Prime Minister and the Minister for External Territories went to Fairbairn to meet the Chief Minister on arrival. Television suitably covered this public acknowledgment of status.

The meeting on 17 January was in a Canberra parliamentary committee room which was well filled by a mass of advisers — those present at the commencement were:

> The Prime Minister
> the Treasurer (Mr Crean)
> the Minister for External Territories (Mr Morrison)
> the Minister for Aboriginal Affairs (Mr Bryant)
> the Chief Minister
> the Secretary, Department of External Territories
> the Secretary, Aboriginal Affairs
> the Deputy Secretary, Prime Minister's Department
> myself
> the Prime Minister's personal private secretary
> the Chief Minister's advisers, Messrs Ritchie, Barnett, Momis, Sarei and Ryan.
> External Territories officers

two representatives of the Attorney-General's Department.

This massive and heterogeneous group was to deal with the Papua New Guinea/Queensland border — or, as the communique put it, the border between Papua New Guinea and Australia. Bryant was there to represent the interests of the Torres Strait Islanders, while the Attorney-General's Department was to ensure that no legal loopholes entered any statement which might give the sovereign state of Queensland any advantages in the International Court of Justice. The Prime Minister seemed to take an inordinately detailed interest in this topic, which interest is reflected in the proportion of the communique devoted to it. Some of this interest was due no doubt to the political incompatibility of Mr Whitlam and the Queensland Premier, Mr Bjelke-Petersen, and to the inflexible attitude of the Queenslanders on the matter of border revision. In other respects the communique outlines the issues discussed except that it does not refer to Bryant's reference to the possibility of establishing the Torres Strait Islands as a special enclave, an idea which was treated with amused disregard by his colleagues.

The Prime Minister and the Chief Minister each stated his position on independence and the careful wording of the communique reflects the public attitudes of each. The Prime Minister, reflecting his newly-assumed national responsibilities, conceded for the first time that the timing for independence would be subject to consultation with the Papua New Guinea Government and to endorsement by the Papua New Guinea House of Assembly as representing the wishes of the people.

For those of us who identified with Papua New Guinea, the future financial relationship with Australia was the most important item on the agenda and earlier in the day Morrison had called the Treasurer, Frank Crean, and, we thought, had obtained his agreement to triennial financing. The draft communique already referred to grants based on a triennial programme, on compensation for loss due to the revaluation of the Australian dollar and to an increased level of aid for 1973–74. However, lunch intervened and the Prime Minister took Morrison, Crean and Somare off to the Lodge to eat while the officials pored over the sentences in the communique relating to the Papua New Guinea/Australian border. We were more than taken aback when the luncheon party returned and told us that all of the financial issues had been settled over lunch. They had been settled to Papua New Guinea's very substantial disadvantage and there seems little doubt but that Crean had taken advantage of the situation to restore the orthodox Treasury approach to Papua New Guinea financing. The positive phrases in the draft communique were replaced by much more nebulous expressions: ". . . aid in terms of finance and skilled manpower would continue . . ."; "Australia also agreed to an urgent examination of the Chief Minister's request for a continuing three-year aid commitment"; ". . . urgent studies by officials of both governments of the effects of revaluation on Papua New Guinea. . .". We resolved that the Prime Minister's visit to Papua New Guinea in February should be the occasion of an attempt to restore the lost ground.

Other topics for discussion at the luncheon were the Chief Minister's difficulties with Bougainville and his problems with his Deputy, John Guise. From this the Prime Minister was rather startled by the Chief Minister's suggestion that he should recommend Knighthoods for Lapun and Guise, as Papua New Guinea recommendations for New Year Honours had been cancelled without reference to Papua New

Guinea. (When a Liberal government came to office Lapun became Papua New Guinea's first indigenous Knight and Guise reached greater elevation as a G.C.M.G. on becoming Governor-General of his country.)

The other subject discussed over lunch was what should happen to the Administrator on self-government and the Chief Minister requested that the present occupant of the post stay until independence. The Prime Minister later asked me to think of a suitable title for the post. Quite apart from what personal motivations there may have been in the Chief Minister's request, he was concerned that a Papua New Guinean replacement for the Administrator might result in the development of a power base for a rival, while the retention of an Australian in the post might be found reassuring by those alarmed at the prospect of early independence.

The Prime Minister, the Chief Minister and the Minister for External Territories concluded the affair with a press conference during which no new issues were raised. Later we had a cheerful dinner at the Lodge during which the Prime Minister confessed to me that although he was a republican, he saw substantial political advantages in the maintenance of links with the monarchy in that it allowed the Prime Minister to nominate a person of his own choice to the post of Governor-General. A Republic might produce a President with an independent power base if produced by a system of combined House of Representatives/Senate vote or by other methods used to determine the holders of such prestigious posts.[2]

Relevant extracts from the communique which was issued after the meeting concluded are given here:

The Prime Minister said that Australia, for her part, would work towards independence in 1974, but that the timing for independence would be subject to consultation with the Papua New Guinea Government and to endorsement by the Papua New Guinea House of Assembly as representing the wishes of the people.

The Prime Minister said that the Australian Government was willing in principle to negotiate the relocation of the border and indeed was keen to do so and would not allow any narrow considerations to obstruct a settlement, but the Government noted that there were constitutional considerations which had to be taken into account and which might delay the matter. Moreover, it would be most reluctant to be a party to any settlement which was not accepted by the Islanders in the respects which affected them.

The Chief Minister reaffirmed that the existing border was unacceptable to his Government but he was confident that it would be possible to reach a solution which would be generally acceptable to all parties including the Islanders. He said that his Government was conscious of the existing rights including land rights of the Islanders and intended that these should be safeguarded in any settlement that might be reached.

The Prime Minister informed the Chief Minister that following self-government and after independence Australian aid in terms of finance and skilled manpower would continue, should that be the wish of the Papua New Guinea Government. Australia also agreed to an urgent examination of the Chief Minister's request for a continuing three-year aid commitment, to begin in the financial year 1974–75 and to be related to Papua New Guinea's Improvement Programme. The nature of this commitment would be determined in the light of circumstances existing at the time the new programme was drawn up.

Security was dealt with separately on 18 January between Papua New Guinea representatives and the Australian Minister for Defence, Lance Barnard and his officers. My summary of the proceedings follows:

Present: Minister for Defence   L.H. Barnard
Minister for Repatriation   Senator R. Bishop
Minister for External   W.L. Morrison
Territories

Chief Minister, Papua New Guinea	M.T. Somare
Chairman, Chiefs of Staff	Admiral Sir Victor Smith
Secretary, Department of External Territories	D.O. Hay
Administrator, Papua New Guinea	L.W. Johnson
Deputy Secretary, Department of Defence	G.E. Blakers

Plus advisers to the above.

The talks were without commitment, discussion was general, there were no undertakings and no decisions.

The Chief Minister made the initial point that Papua New Guinea's principal preoccupation was internal security and that the police force in its present state would have difficulty in ensuring the security of the State in the future. From this it became apparent that measures would have to be taken to strengthen the police, both qualitatively and quantitatively, or expand very greatly the internal security role of the defence forces. Discussion then centred on two main topics:

1. The respective roles of police and defence forces.
2. The level of support the Australian Government might be prepared to give to Papua New Guinea's security forces.

1. *Roles of Defence and Police Forces*

Barnard was firm in his view that he hoped Papua New Guinea would retain a small defence force with the principal role of defence against external aggression. He implied that this should be maintained on generally orthodox lines so that there could be quick and easy cooperation with Australian forces if necessary. Both he and Morrison expressed anxiety that in the period until independence the defence force might get involved in internal police actions. When it was pointed out that under the present direction, aid to the civil power was provided only in extreme emergencies and that in these circumstances the Army resorted to the most stringent control measures, Barnard readily agreed that there should be gradations in army intervention and in the control measures used. He admitted the need for joint police/army training in crowd control and asked his advisers to bring recommendations to his notice. However, it was clear that both Barnard and Morrison thought that Australian interests would best be served by the building up of police strength, if necessary at the expense of the defence force, rather than by the defence force assuming an active internal security role. Their preference clearly was for the maintenance of an orthodox defence establishment.

The Chief Minister implied acceptance of this point of view, subject to assurances of adequate Australian support for whatever forces would be required to maintain adequate internal security. Morrison and Somare then each advanced views on the nature of the internal security force required and seemed to agree that a paramilitary force based possibly on the existing police mobile squads would be suitable. Parallels were drawn with the Malaysian para-military forces. It was pointed out that the existing mobile squads might well be a suitable base, given better training and leadership. Barnard seemed to concur with the suggestion that training and leadership assistance could be provided from defence force resources and that experienced army NCOs could be incorporated in this force. There was an appreciation of the need to strengthen the mobile squads immediately as the development and organization of what might ultimately become a separate internal security field force would take some time.

2. *Level of Support*

It was accepted by all that the maintenance of a defence force with orthodox objectives would require a very high level of Australian financial assistance and that it was very much in the Australian interest to also ensure internal peace and stability in Papua New Guinea.

What seemed to emerge as a consensus was that

Australian aid would continue to be available to support security forces (police, field force and defence force) at about the present manpower level and with about the total financial resources presently devoted to these forces, except that the Papua New Guinea Government would be expected to find the money to pay the wages of the indigenous members of the defence force. The sums of money discussed were that Australia would continue to provide for defence force costs less about $3.5 million, which was the estimated bill for soldiers' pay, and to assist the police at approximately the same level as at present ($8 million was mentioned as the sum presently provided from the Development Grant but no one was able to verify this). On present expenditure patterns this would mean total Australian assistance of about $30 million.

A total manpower figure of about 6,000 was mentioned and Barnard seemed to regard this as a ceiling. The development of a police field force of greater numbers than at present would therefore be at the expense of the defence force or of the regular police. I would not regard this as a firm view and there appeared to be room for a good deal of flexibility.

Summary

Although there were no conclusions, the salient points appear to be:

1. Development of a police field force of a para-military nature.
2. Maintenance of an orthodox defence force.
3. Defence force assistance in the development of a para-military police force based on mobile squads both in training and in actual manpower.
4. Joint training exercises police/army to meet emergency situations pending the development of a fully effective field force.
5. Australian financial assistance at about the present level for the total security forces.
6. Papua New Guinea's obligation to provide for the pay of the indigenous members of the defence force.

Comments

> If the discussions are taken to their logical conclusion,
> there would be a total manpower ceiling for the
> security forces of 6,000 plus. These would be divided
> between three forces each with a differing role —
> Defence Force, Police Field Force, Regular Police — but
> with provision for co-operation in particular circum-
> stances and presumably a system of personnel inter-
> change and a high degree of commonality of equip-
> ment, supply etc.[3]

The orgy of summitry reached a climax and a conclusion in February when the new Australian Prime
Minister paid a triumphant visit to Papua New Guinea.
The objects of the visit were set out by the Department
of External Territories as follows:

- to enable the Prime Minister to renew, in Papua
  New Guinea, his acquaintances with Ministers of
  the National Coalition Government and to discuss
  with them in private any particular matters which
  might be troubling them;
- to calm, by public statements of the policy of the
  new Australian Government at the highest level,
  the anxieties still felt by some Papua New Guinea
  leaders that Australia was forcing Papua New
  Guinea towards early independence in order to
  reduce Australian aid obligations;
- to indicate, in public and private statements,
  Australia's policies towards the region in which
  Australia and Papua New Guinea would find themselves independent neighbours before very long.

The Prime Minister arrived in Port Moresby on 18
February accompanied by Mrs Whitlam, daughter
Kathie, Morrison and sundry support staff. The
Whitlams stayed with us and one could hardly have had
more pleasant guests.

The three days devoted to the visit were packed with
consultations and official functions, but in the talks

most time was spent on the sensitive topic of Australian financial aid, about which we in Papua New Guinea had received uncertain signals from Canberra. We were anxious to know if the new Australian Government's pocket lay close to its heart. Julius Chan, the Finance Minister, presented a formidable list of needs; first, he requested an immediate budget supplement to assist Papua New Guinea to meet unforeseen expenditure resulting from cyclone damage, a famine in the highlands and the appreciation of the Australian dollar. Second, he sought an aid commitment over the next three years. Next, he wanted an Australian Government guarantee of Papua New Guinea's overseas loans, and finally, assistance in building up financial reserves. He also put in a bid for tariff concessions for Papua New Guinea products entering Australia.

The Prime Minister, unprepared for such comprehensive requests, played a straight bat: "some of the matters were too technical or precise for him to answer immediately. Others required Cabinet decision and he was not in a position to commit his government on them. Some were also technical matters arising primarily within the area of responsibility of Mr Crean, the Commonwealth Treasurer,"[4] but he did offer hope that Australian aid might underwrite Papua New Guinea's three-year Improvement Programme as it had underwritten the previous Five-Year-Plan.

Having shelved finance for the time being the meeting turned its attention to the timing of self-government. Somare scared the Prime Minister when he told him that the Constitutional Planning Committee, which was procrastinating to some purpose, would not be able to produce recommendations to be enacted before the agreed date for self-government, 1 December that year. Both Whitlam and Morrison jumped to the unpalatable conclusion that this might

mean deferring the self-government date and a consequent delay in the achievement of independence. "His
party stated that Papua New Guinea ought to be independent during the life of the current Australian
parliament. He would be failing to carry out his undertakings to the Australian electorate if this was not
achieved."[5] I intervened to point out that the Papua
New Guinea Government had no intention of delaying
self-government and saw no difficulty in the transfer of
power prior to final conclusions on the ultimate shape
of the Papua New Guinea constitution. It should be said
that the Constitutional Planning Committee didn't see it
that way; they were alarmed that the transfer of power
before a home-grown constitution was in place might
entrench existing practices and privileges.

The next item was also a difficult one. Somare made a
formal request for the transfer of the police and responsibility for internal security. There was a marked reluctance on Australia's part to surrender these powers at
this early stage. Whitlam expressed his Government's
fears:

> The topic was important to his Government as
> Australia was responsible to the United Nations for law
> and order and would technically remain so until the
> Trusteeship Agreement was dissolved at Independence.
> . . . Under the previous government the Australian
> Army had been called out. This Government was very
> reluctant for law and order to be in the hands of anyone
> other than the police. The Joint Defence Force had
> Australian officers and his Government would never
> live it down if the Australian Army was involved in the
> shooting of Papua New Guineans.[6]

A deal of the reply rather begged the question of the
transfer of control of the police. John Guise pressed the
issue, which drew from Whitlam the assurance that
there was no inclination by his Government to drag its

feet on this. There the matter rested. Somare had not really expected an immediate agreement but the demand was on the table.

The final matter of importance discussed was the vexed question of the Australia/Papua New Guinea border in the Torres Straits, on which no proposal had been made. All that could be said was a rehearsal of the obstacles in the way of a resolution of an acceptable boundary. It was only some years later that an agreement was reached.

Other than these business matters the Prime Minister attended and spoke at a graduation ceremony at the University of Papua New Guinea at which UPNG's first graduates in Medicine were presented. In addition, there were five graduates with Science degrees, four graduates in Economics, twenty in Education and seven in Law. Whitlam spoke on "Unity and Culture in Papua New Guinea" and, as far as Papua New Guinea was concerned, the central paragraphs of the speech were:

> I know these ideals of unity and a distinctive national culture are dear to the hearts of the Chief Minister and his colleagues. Your Chief Minister explained to me . . . his wish to preserve and develop the cultural heritage of your people and a feeling for your nation's history and way of life. He therefore asked my Government to give special Australian aid for a national programme for cultural development. . . . I am pleased to announce that beginning in the next financial year we will assist your programme with a grant of $15 million over the next five years.[7]

The grant was to relocate and develop the Museum, to expand the already active Creative Arts Centre and assist in the development of an Institute of Papua New Guinea cultures. The Prime Minister could hardly have made a more welcome announcement. With the assistance of the grant a fine museum was developed and the Creative Arts Centre became a focus for cultural creativity in Papua New Guinea. I was reminded that some years earlier I had successfully persuaded Michael Somare, then leader of the Pangu opposition in the second House of Assembly, to take on the chairmanship of the Museum's governing council.

At the conclusion of the graduation there was a feast in the University hall to which relatives of students were invited. They set upon the food with such gusto that the official party missed out and on returning to our house the Whitlams and my wife and I were reduced to making sandwiches and eating ice-cream in our kitchen.

On the same day the Prime Minister's party had made a flying visit to Goroka in the Eastern Highlands, where Whitlam was greeted by a splendid display of the various tribes in traditional dress, all wearing their best plumes. The conservatives of the Eastern Highlands District, at this time by far the majority of the population, seized the occasion to present a petition to the Prime Minister expressing their disquiet at the course of events. Key paragraphs were:

> Do not forget, Sir, that education was not started in the Highlands until 1953, and the few of our members who are educated are our first, not necessarily our best, and their views are not necessarily our views. We are not educated, and our members are naive in government, but we do not lack common sense and we understand that progress to Independence must be based on a sound economy. We are afraid that our present economy is in jeopardy, and our Ministers do nothing to rectify the situation. In fact they seem bent on destroying it. . . . We do not fear the approach of independence as a natural follow-through of successful self-government but we do object to setting a date for Independence as we do not know if our government of the day will be capable of fulfilling the responsibilities of Independence by that time.

The freedom of operation the Australian Government has allowed our Coalition Government has enabled us to see that our Government is not responsible or mature enough to handle a happy and beneficial Independence.

We oppose your Government setting a date for Independence for the above mentioned reasons. We are vigorously opposed to our present Government setting dates for Independence because it is their decision, not ours, and we have no confidence in their ability to handle Independence.[8]

But the most important speeches were then delivered at a formal dinner. The Chief Minister and the Leader of the Opposition each welcomed the Prime Minister and each emphasized the same point; that an independence date should be reached by the decision of the people of Papua New Guinea and that it should not be precipitated by pressure from Australia. Somare said

my government feels that we should not set a date for Independence until we have achieved self-government and have had time to adjust to self-government. We realize the external pressures on Australia to set an early date for independence and we realize the internal pressures for Australia to end its colonial role. At the same time my Government has strong pressures on it to resist a too-sudden transition to Independence. However the Prime Minister has assured me that he will consult my Government and the House of Assembly on the date for Independence. If both our countries adopt a realistic attitude and take into account each other's problems I am sure that we will find a solution that is mutually acceptable.[9]

Toliman was rather more explicit but began with what Whitlam accepted as a compliment, though that may not have been the intention:

I doubt if any single man has had a greater influence in speeding up the changes in our country in the past few years than yourself . . . Australia cleared the way for the establishment of this Parliament in 1964 with the promise — and the Australian Labor Party publicly endorsed that promise — that our own House of Assembly should make all the important decisions on the way of life and future of our people. . . . We trust that the good sense and good will of the Australian Government will not prematurely force us into Independence. While this could resolve pressures on Australia's Government and meet its short term interests, in the long run there could be a very real risk of destroying the friendship and trust which now exists between us.[10]

Whitlam responded, dwelling on three themes, independence, aid and unity. On the first of these he restated his Government's position, though reaffirming that Papua New Guinea's resolution of important issues "should be by recorded vote and by a substantial majority representative of the nation as a whole". This in fact was a repetition of the agreement in 1972 as to how a decision on the date for self-government should be reached. But he also qualified that affirmation: "I cannot stress too often that the decision for Independence is not only a decision about Papua New Guinea. It is about Australia, and Australia's view of her own proper role in the world. Australia is no longer willing to be the ruler of a colony. And my Government is determined to divest itself of that role in the lifetime of the present Australian parliament."[11] In effect he gave Papua New Guinea the deadline for Independence at the end of 1975, given the expectation of a normal three-year for the newly elected Labor government.

As for aid he gave the usual rather nebulous assurances which bore the influence of the Australian Treasury. "The Australian Government has decided to give the Papua New Guinea Government an assurance of continuing aid over the period of the three year

Improvement Programme beginning in 1974 . . . Papua New Guinea will have the first call on our substantially increased foreign aid programme."

But he devoted his strongest words to the subject of unity, against the rising centrifugal forces released by the Bougainville independence movement.

> My Government's policy, . . . is to hand over our remaining powers to a national and representative Government, freely elected by the people of the whole of Papua New Guinea and able to represent the wishes of the majority of the people. Relations between our two countries will be conducted through the National Government in Canberra and the Central Government of Papua New Guinea. Australian aid will be allocated solely through the Central Government. On 20 December 1971 the United Nations General Assembly, by resolution, urged Australia to discourage separatist movements and to ensure that the unity of Papua New Guinea is preserved throughout the period leading up to independence. On 14 December last year the General Assembly again reaffirmed "the importance of ensuring the preservation of unity".[12]

The tumult and the shouting were over, the Prime Minister and party departed. Although it had evoked not much more than a re-stating of well known positions, it had served a useful purpose in assuring many in Papua New Guinea that the Australian Prime Minister of 1973 was not the ogre they had encountered in 1970–71. He had guaranteed the continuation of Australian aid, though not saying how much it might be. He had agreed that the House of Assembly should nominate the independence day, though suggesting strongly that it should be before the end of 1975. What is more, contrary to his earlier visits, he had been courteous to all shades of political opinion in Papua New Guinea. The Whitlam undertakings were confirmed by the Governor-General when he opened the newly-elected

Australian parliament a week or so later, on 27
February 1973. "My Government will move with all
due speed towards the creation of an independent,
united Papua New Guinea within the life of this parliament. My Government is deeply committed by the
clearest pledges to continue substantial economic aid to
an independent Papua New Guinea . . . Legislation will
be introduced to provide for self-government on 1
December 1973 or as soon as possible thereafter".[13]
There was a bit of grumbling about Whitlam's stand-
over tactics on an independence date but Somare was
not displeased because Whitlam was making the
running on this sensitive topic and the Papua New
Guinea Government felt free to pursue its own policies
without the prospect of undue Australian interference.

Immediately following this prestigious occasion there
was a low-key commemoration, on 21 February, of the
naming of Port Moresby and the harbour on which the
city stands, Fairfax Harbour. Captain John Moresby of
the Royal Navy brought his ship into the harbour on 21
February 1873 and promptly commemorated the occasion by honouring his father Admiral Sir Fairfax
Moresby. Captain Moresby may have been preceded
by Torres more than two hundred years earlier, and the
claim that he had discovered Port Moresby is hardly
tenable when the site was already well populated by the
Papuan people. Of the people of Hanuabada, for
instance, Moresby confided to his journal:

> Its inhabitants, numbering perhaps 800 of all ages, were
> well fed contented-looking people. The women seemed
> to busy themselves much in pottery and moulded clay
> into large globe-shaped jars which they baked slowly
> amongst the embers of wood fires. . . . I have partaken
> of a vegetable porridge cooked in them [the jars] con-
> sisting of mangrove fruit, taro and yams with coconut
> shredded over all, and found it excellent.[14]

The Port Moresby City Council gave thought to some recognition of the centenary of Moresby's arrival. A re-enactment of the landing was suggested but there was a contrary opinion that the arrival of colonial influence in Papua was hardly a cause for celebration. Eventually it was decided that the event would be commemorated by a public lecture where the platform was shared by Nigel Oram and Ken Inglis, both from the University of Papua New Guinea, the latter being the foundation Professor of History, and at that time, the Vice-Chancellor of the University. The event had such patronage that it had to be repeated the following night for the overflow. Among those present was the great-grandson of Captain Moresby's brother. He had come to Papua New Guinea for the occasion.

The lectures were incorporated into a booklet: "John Moresby and Port Moresby, A Centenary View",[15] and in it Inglis, discussing the surprising popularity of the lectures, comments:

> At question time it was made vividly clear that many people had come not out of an antiquarian or sentimental interest in the events of 1873, or to spend a more salubrious evening than the tavern or club could offer, but in the hope that they would be given information of direct use in 1973. Did Moresby observe any people living on Daugo (Yule's Fisherman's Islets)? The question was asked by one man and pursued by others who had been, and still were, engaged in legal disputes about rights to use the island. Other questions about Moresby's journey had similar purposes.

NOTES

1. Record of press conference, 7 December 1972, PP.
2. Record of meeting, Somare and Whitlam, in Canberra, 17 January 1973, summarized 22 January 1973, PP.

3. Record of meeting, Somare and Barnard, in Canberra, 18 January 1973, summarized 22 January 1973.
4. Quote from the Papua New Guinea official record of the talks, Port Moresby, PP.
5. Ibid.
6. Ibid. It should be noted that a "call out" had been authorized but not implemented.
7. "Unity and Culture in Papua New Guinea", speech by the Prime Minister, E.G. Whitlam, at a graduation ceremony, UPNG, Port Moresby, February 1973, PP.
8. Petition, Goroka, February 1973, PP.
9. Copy of speech, February 1973, among PP.
10. Ibid.
11. Ibid.
12. Ibid.
13. Reprinted in *Select Policy Statements on Papua New Guinea* AGPS, Canberra, 1973.
14. "Discoveries in Eastern New Guinea", *Journal of the Royal Historical Society* XLV (1975).
15. "John Moresby and Port Moresby, A Centenary View", Papua New Guinea Government Printer, Port Moresby, June 1974.

14

SHEDDING THE BONDS

The rest of 1973 was full of action accompanied by a great deal of rhetoric, the latter being provided in plenty by members of the Constitutional Planning Committee, particularly Momis and Kaputin. The Constitutional Planning Committee (CPC), first set up in September 1972, had an ambitious target date of July 1973 for presenting its recommendations to the House of Assembly so that the necessary adoption procedures could be completed before self-government in December. The Committee soon fell hopelessly behind in meeting its objective, in part, because of the determination of its Vice-Chairman, Momis, that the Constitution should be thoroughly home-grown, free of any colonial taint, though, of its permanent support staff of six, four were Australians. The Committee suffered a further setback when Professor Jim Davidson died leaving a considerable gap in the experienced advice available to the Committee. The CPC developed as a separate pressure group seeking to inhibit all Government action that might pre-empt the Committee's recommendations.

However it did come up with its First Interim Report in September 1973. Paragraph 10 of that report sets out the Committee's position:

These transfers of power, however, raised a serious problem for the Committee — that of possible pre-emption of options that might otherwise be open to the Committee to recommend. The Australian and Papua New Guinea Governments have been primarily interested in transferring powers as smoothly and quickly as possible, and generally in accordance with the Australian or some other pre-conceived system. The Committee, however, has been interested primarily on the extent to which such a system might be appropriate to the circumstances of Papua New Guinea. The emphasis on quantitative transfer has been a form of neo-colonialism involving an excessive carryover of Australian methods and concepts. The Committee has been anxious to preclude the institutionalization of power in ways which might be very difficult to change later should this be found desirable.[1]

Other than this, the Report referred briefly to the separatist movements in Bougainville and Papua, reporting, in the former case, that "although Committee members were made aware that secession remains a real issue in Bougainville there was no call for it at the meetings held on the island. The people seemed genuinely prepared to explore the possibility of satisfying their aspirations through a form of district government",[2] and in Papua, "as elsewhere there was a call for some degree of autonomy with emphasis on local identity, but not separation".[3]

Arising from its meetings with the people the report summarized majority views that, first, only single citizenship should be allowed (Australians who were permanent residents naturally favoured dual citizenship); and second, that a system of district government should be introduced. The citizenship issue aroused most heat as initially the radicals on the CPC wished to make it almost exclusively a privilege for autochthones by specifying that citizenship should be available only to those with at least three indigenous grandparents, while draconian regulations to apply to naturalization procedures were also proposed. Ultimately the automatic citizenship requirement was for at least one indigenous grandparent, which took a lot of anxious potential citizens off the hook, including some members of parliament, not to mention the leader of the People's Progress Party, Julius Chan, later to be Papua New Guinea's second Prime Minister, who at that time was an Australian citizen.

The laboured progress of the Constitutional Planning Committee necessitated a review of the political processes required to achieve self-government. In May, Morrison came to Port Moresby when, in consultation with Somare, Momis, myself and four CPC members, a decision was reached that there should be a two-stage process. The press release set out the prospective timetable:

December 1973: Formal self-government will be introduced by means of amendments to the *Papua New Guinea Act* passed by the Australian Parliament. The Act will then reflect in law the present situation of virtual self-government.

February 1974: The final report and draft constitution recommended by the Constitutional Planning Committee will be tabled in the Papua New Guinea House of Assembly. The Constitution will provide for all major aspects of the system of government and will include provisions for the transition to independence.

April 1974: The House of Assembly will meet in special session to consider and adopt the Constitution. Following the adoption by the House of Assembly of the Constitution it would be reserved for the consent of the Governor-General.

May 1974:   The Australian Parliament will consider further amendments to the
Papua New Guinea Act to remove
from that Act those parts which provide for the internal constitution of
Papua New Guinea and which have
been included in the Papua New
Guinea constitution as adopted by
the House of Assembly. Following
the passing of the amendments to the
Papua New Guinea Act, the Governor-
General will be requested to assent to
these amendments and to the Papua
New Guinea Constitution.[4]

Everyone's plans and expectations were based on the
estimate that independence would come in the latter
part of 1974, possibly on National Day in September,
though in fact, it was a year beyond that date before independence was achieved.

In the year leading up to self-government thoughtful
Papua New Guineans were striving to assert their national status in a variety of ways. There was a conscious
effort to discard the colonial past and to seek help and
advice from elsewhere. "De-Australianization" was the
uncomfortable name given to the process. The Papua
New Guinea Government began to follow the established practice of the University and the Institute of
Technology in its recruitment, though indeed this was
in part a necessity as Australians no longer found
employment conditions in Papua New Guinea as attractive as in the past. The Government, for instance,
deliberately excluded well qualified and experienced
Australians for the top job of economic planner and
ultimately engaged a young Canadian, David Beatty, at
an inflated salary. At last in the House of Assembly
wigs were discarded by the Speaker and the House
clerks and members decided that jackets were no longer
necessary in the House Chamber.

Nonetheless Australians still remained in influential positions and few Papua New Guineans had reached the summit as Heads of Departments. I sought to remedy this situation by implementing the process of termination of positions under the provisions of the Employment Security Scheme (ESS) which provided generous separation terms for those whose positions were localized. Three Australian departmental heads had departed by mid-year, McKinnon in Education, Syme in Health and Newby in Information. Health and Education had always been in the forefront of the localization process and were fortunate in having a number of Papua New Guinean officers capable of filling the top positions adequately. By mid-1973 there were five indigenous Heads of Departments and Sere Pitoi was Chairman of the Public Service Board. It was still a very small proportion for a country shortly to be self-governing. In the Public Service as a whole, Australians were taking advantage of the ESS provisions and departing more rapidly than the Government had foreseen. Serious gaps were appearing, particularly in the technical and professional fields where alternative employment opportunities in Australia were available. Papua New Guinea began to look seriously at recruitment possibilities in other countries to fill the many positions for which local officers were not available. A preliminary recruiting mission visited the Philippines which later resulted in a substantial number of Filipinos joining the Papua New Guinea work force.

Somare was not immune to criticism for his reliance on Australian advisors. He had been strongly supported by an informal group of able young men led by Tony Voutas who had played a major role in the development of the Pangu Pati. Other leading figures in the group were Paul Ryan, Thos Barnett and Mark Lynch whom I had earlier chosen to set up the Department of the Chief Minister. Other charter members were Ross Garnaut, Peter Fitzpatrick and Jim Fingleton, all academics. Papua New Guinean members of the group around Somare were Moi Avei, Charles Lepani and Rabie Namaliu. It was a happy blend of experience, brains and initiative and did a great deal to keep the National Coalition Government afloat with Somare at its head. Pressure on Somare ultimately led to the departure of his closest adviser, Tony Voutas.

In 1973, for the first time, Papua New Guinea's foreign relations became a subject for discussion and concern among local parliamentarians and the better informed segments of the population. As I have previously indicated, we had already initiated a diplomatic training scheme and had our first graduates, Tony Siaguru and Ben Sabumei, attached to Australian overseas missions. Siaguru later became the first in-digenous head of Papua New Guinea's Department of Foreign Relations and Trade, which Department had been formally established in April 1970. In 18 November 1973 I summarized the situation as I saw it:

> There is a natural desire to be free of the over-dominant presence of Australia, but, nonetheless, a continued sense of dependence. Whatever foreign exploitation Papua New Guineans have suffered from and whatever aspects of racial discrimination have offended their humanity, it has been Australians who have inflicted it. At the same time, most of the better things Papua New Guineans have enjoyed have come from the same source. It might be said that there is a relationship at three levels; first of all at the individual level where there is a great deal of trust and confidence, second, a Papua New Guinean attitude towards Australians en masse, which is antipathetic; and third, towards an Australian Government, where Papua New Guinea is assertive and aggressive while being quite confident of continued Australian support. Certainly the Papua New Guinean Government has every confidence in continu-

ing large-scale Australian aid for as long as it is required. There appears to be reason for confidence that a satisfactory fraternal relationship can be established and maintained though Australia should not take Papua New Guinea for granted.

Papua New Guinea is only now becoming conscious of the inevitability of establishing a pattern of relationships with other countries and presently, apart from other Pacific nations, it recognizes only the importance of Indonesia and Japan. The Pacific relationship was activated by participation in the South Pacific Commission and by the development of regular pan-Pacific athletic contests — the South Pacific Games. It is probably the latter which had most impact on the majority of Papua New Guineans and, in particular, the 1969 Games held in Port Moresby. Whatever the cause, Papua New Guineans recognize and cultivate what might be called their ethnic affinity with the rest of the Pacific and expect to assume a leadership role, at least among the Melanesian peoples.

Papua New Guinea's attitude towards Indonesia, first developed through fear, no doubt strengthened by Australian apprehensions at the time of confrontation, grew into hostility over the period of the Act of Free Choice. Since that time there has been a considerable change in public attitudes through a recognition that one has little option but to be friendly with a neighbouring giant. The efforts of both the Australian and Indonesian Governments to reassure Papua New Guinea have also been effective in inducing changed attitudes.

The feeling towards Japan is rather more ambivalent and springs from a widely held conviction that the Japanese are out to exploit Papua New Guinea for their own ends and that they will be too much of a handful to be controlled effectively. Japanese commercial penetration on a large scale is accepted as a regrettable but inevitable fact of life. Most Papua New Guineans with any understanding of Papua New Guinea's position in the world are doubtful as to the efficacy of investment controls and other protective devices. It is highly desirable to maintain close Government-to-Government links to control possible commercial excesses. Papua New Guinea regards Australia as a source of support in its relations with Japan.

For the rest there is great respect for the efficiency of the Singaporeans and dislike of Malaysians, who are regarded as patronizing. Europe and America are too remote for serious consideration and China has attracted attention only from small professional groups (e.g. medicos). The Philippines is known only as a source of a beer now manufactured in Port Moresby and as a country which may be able to fill in the gaps in professional and technical manpower.

One related event was the visit in November of Indonesia's Foreign Minister Adam Malik and his party, to sign an agreement on the border between Papua New Guinea and Irian Jaya. Dr and Mrs Malik were pleasant guests at our house. There were cordial exchanges between the representatives of the two governments, and some relief on the Papua New Guinea side that a boundary had been firmly delineated and was now to be formally ratified. At a dinner in his honour Malik had some reassuring things to say:

Signing the Indonesia-Papua New Guinea border agreement. Seated from left: Les Johnson, Albert Maori Kiki, Michael Somare, Adam Malik.

From the outset Indonesia has consistently supported the cause of full independence for Papua New Guinea. Now on the eve of self-government leading towards complete independence I would like to reiterate that the Indonesian people and Government wish nothing more than to see a stable, secure and prosperous Papua New Guinea assume her rightful place among the family of sovereign States. . . . Indonesia, on her part, will do everything within her capabilities to work for a harmonious relationship of fraternal and mutually beneficial co-operation with Papua New Guinea, and to lay at rest whatever misconceptions or unfounded apprehensions there may still linger in the minds of some segments of our people towards one another.[5]

Closer to home what was most strongly desired, and frequently spoken of, was a change of direction in economic policy, to equalize the distribution of wealth and opportunity. Impetus to this was given by a report on appropriate development strategies for Papua New Guinea prepared by the Overseas Development Group of the University of East Anglia, commissioned by the United Nations Development Programme through the World Bank. The report, sometimes referred to as the Faber Report, after the team leader, overturned the gospel according to the World Bank survey of 1964, in which the central theme had been expressed thus: "To obtain maximum benefit from the development effort, expenditures and manpower should be concentrated on areas and on activities where the prospective return is highest.[6]

Referring to this earlier report the Faber team had this to say: "But whatever the merits of the past programme the consultants would wish to record that they had found that the need for a marked change of emphasis was now widely recognized by those in public life and in the public service both within the Papua New Guinea Administration and within the Commonwealth Government."[7]

In brief, the longer term objectives set out in the report were:

1. Increased local, indigenous control of the economy and the indigenization of many forms of economic activity.
2. An emphasis on growth of "income to nationals".
3. Major increases in the opportunities for employment and more particularly for income-generating self-employment.
4. A comparatively greater emphasis upon rural development.

The report further noted that "the existence of large income disparities in close juxtaposition to each other is, in itself, likely to be a source of economic ill-being, because it will give rise to wants, dissatisfactions and possibly a feeling of permanent inferiority which the person on the lower income will normally be quite unable to remedy".[8]

The report was the springboard from which the Somare Government launched its Improvement Program, later known as the Eight-Point-Plan. It followed closely the tenor of the Faber Report. Indigenization of the economy, equalization of income, support for small-scale business activity, emphasis on rural production, a self-reliant economy and, curiously enough, a word in favour of equality for women and their participation in economic and social activity (undoubtedly a Voutas insertion). Papua New Guinea women working their gardens, carrying the firewood, tending the pigs, looking after the children would have been surprised to find that they were not yet considered to be active participants in the rural economy, though they would certainly have agreed that their status was not yet equal to that of their menfolk. In his statement to the House of Assembly Somare said:

"The new aims reflect a deliberate choice by the Government. We choose to build a nation where economic development reaches all of the people, not just a favoured few who have good jobs in government or industry. We choose to build a nation where men and women who live in the villages get a fair share of the rewards of progress. We choose to build a nation where there are no great differences between rich and poor. And we choose to build a nation able to provide for itself, a nation able to plan for itself, a nation able to stand on its own and face the rest of the world with dignity and pride."[9]

The realization of these fine sentiments seemed far off but at least the rapid departure of Australian Public Servants and their replacement by somewhat less affluent Papua New Guineans was a small step in the right direction.

Throughout the climactic year of 1973 the House of Assembly remained an uncertain base of support for the Somare Government in its implementation of new policies. Somare's early difficulties in 1973 were with his Cabinet, for he still had some unfulfilled promises. In putting together the Coalition in April 1972 he had promised the Mataungans a Ministry and he also had a long-standing commitment to Pita Lus — a fellow Sepik, a founding member of the Pangu Pati and one of the few members who had served in all three parliaments. Perhaps his dilemma and the resolution of it are best left to my own account of it, made at the time. Perhaps the account is over-long in relation to the significance of the events, but I hope it does convey some contemporary flavour of the politics of the day.

In his Ministerial reconstruction Somare had a number of objectives, some of which he made no serious attempt to realize. Of this latter group was a hope that he might be able to dump Ministerial embarrassments Sasakila Moses and Paulus Arek. However, given the difficult and tortuous process of getting rid of a Minister and the lack of any convention that a Minister would resign on the request of the Chief Minister, there was little hope of accomplishing this end. His next objective was to loosen the hold of the PPP on the economic Ministries and strengthen the position of the Pangu Pati in the Cabinet and Ministry. As part of this deal, he was prepared to try to depose Guise as Deputy Chief Minister and substitute Chan — at the expense to Chan of his existing overlordship of economic policy. Further, he wanted to get Poe of the PPP out of Foreign Relations and Trade to a post where his frail talents were less exposed to the outside world.

In all of these he failed. Moses and Arek remained immovable and lengthy negotiations and numerous Ministerial lists circulating briskly in the confined circles of the Coalition leadership failed to produce any agreement. Perhaps of least consequence were the names of the additional Ministers to be appointed and it was generally assumed that Kaputin of the Mataungan Association, Lus and one other would be the beneficiaries. Given the strength of highlands feeling and the desire to strengthen the National Coalition Government's position there, it was likely that the third place would go to a highlander; Kaupa, a literate Chimbu, but with little else to commend him, was on the early lists but was ultimately replaced by Yano Belo, an illiterate Southern Highlander, the only member from that District in the Coalition camp. He came there, not by conviction, but out of pique as the United Party had overlooked his claim to membership of their front bench and had chosen two other Southern Highlanders, Wabiria and Yuwi, both from the Huri people.

Kaputin, Lus and Belo was not a very attractive package and there was going to be obvious difficulty with the Ministerial Nominations Committee and with the House in getting acceptance. Kaputin's relative aloofness from other members and his radical views made him suspect, while many members of the Pangu Pati failed to see why a Mataungan Association member, who not infrequently voted against the Government, should win a Ministry. Lus' behaviour in the House was at times erratic and Belo's appointment was obviously one of political convenience.

Meanwhile argument on re-allocation of portfolios proceeded, or failed to proceed. Somare had in mind injecting Kaputin into an economic portfolio and had one called "Trade and Commerce" in mind. This would mean the transfer of Poe to something less prestigious. Chan resisted. It had been decided to create a new portfolio, "Justice", with Guise in mind as Minister. Guise would have been compliant if he could have taken with him some of his existing responsibilities, notably Corrective Institutions, and retained his Deputy Chief Ministership. Without these he refused to budge — indeed wept at the prospect of change. Somare surrendered. It was also necessary to soothe Kavali's ego by giving him a portfolio of policy content instead of Public Works and this entailed more shuffling.

Ultimately an uneasy compromise was reached. Poe had his responsibilities curtailed and finished up as Minister for Trade and Industry while Kiki became Minister for Defence and Foreign Relations. Kavali took over Lands, Kiki's old portfolio. This left Justice, Works and Police vacant for three new Ministers, yet to be formally approved by the House after scrutiny and recommendation by myself and the Ministerial Nominations Committee. The names before us were those of Kaputin, Belo and Lus.

This agreement was reached during the third and final week of the June/July meeting of the House of Assembly and on the evening of Tuesday 5 July, I was requested to convene the Ministerial Nominations Committee. The following day I did this formally but an immediate difficulty arose as the Chairman of the Committee, Obed Boas, had departed for Rabaul and regulations required that all members of the Committee had to be present during its deliberations. Hasty messages followed Boas to Rabaul and he undertook to return immediately to arrive about midday on Thursday. The meeting was convened at 1.30 p.m. on Thursday only to find that another member, Kavali, had gone home to bed sick. The meeting was deferred until 5 p.m. to meet at Kavali's sickbed. This time unanimity was reached on Kaputin, Belo and Lus and the Chairman was rushed to my house to get my concurrence. This obtained, and a formal note despatched to the Speaker, it was possible for Somare to give notice of motion to seek House approval that evening. Debate on the motion followed the next afternoon, the last day of the meeting, and there were early indications of trouble when the Chief Minister attempted to cut off the standard grievance debate and to proceed with Government business. He failed to get the numbers and had to wait until the afternoon.

Meanwhile the Opposition had circulated a skilful amendment to the Government motion on Ministries. The motion read:

> "That this House nominates for appointment to Ministerial Office the following persons whose names are on the list of members submitted to this House after consultation between His Honour the Administrator and the Ministerial Nominations Committee of this House as the list of elected Members eligible to be nominated by the House for such appointment, namely Mr Yano Belo, Mr John Kaputin and Mr Pita Lus."

The amendment moved by Toliman was:

> "That the motion be amended by deleting all the words after 'that this House', and inserting 'while not refusing to nominate for appointment to Ministerial Offices the following persons, being all the persons whose names are on the list of elected Members submitted to this House after consultation between His Honour the Administrator and the Ministerial Nominations Committee of this House as the list of elected Members eligible to be nominated by the House for such appointment namely Mr Yano Belo, Mr John Kaputin, and Mr Pita Lus, before doing so requests these names be referred back to His Honour the Administrator and the Ministerial Nominations Committee for further consideration together with the names of Mr Michael Pondros, Mr John Kaupa, Father John Momis, Mr John Maneke, Mr Naipuri Maina and Mr Tom Koraea."

The six men mentioned in the amendment, all supporters of the NCG, were young, ambitious and certainly would have pretensions to ministerial office,
except perhaps Momis who, as Deputy Chairman of
the Constitutional Planning Committee, already
enjoyed the perquisites and salary of a Minister. The
amendment certainly put heavy pressure on their
loyalty to the Government.

Debate on the amendment proceeded all afternoon
with the numbers early in the afternoon appearing to
favour the Opposition though two attempts to cut
debate and vote on the amendment failed. The Government sought to rally its forces and despatched cars and
staff far and wide to gather in absentees. Perhaps
modesty kept Kaputin and Belo absent from the House
throughout the afternoon but others were absent for
more personal reasons. The amendment was brought to
the vote at 5 p.m. when the Government judged it had
accumulated the numbers. It had, but only just, as the
amendment was lost 28–25. Kaupa abstained and other
notable absentees from the Government supporters
were Mola, Olewale, Kaputin, Maneke, Poe, Diria,
Mona, Pondros, Boas, Tammur and Koraea while Sing-
geri voted with the Opposition. It will be noted that
four of the Government supporters named in the
amendment failed to vote. Turi Wari, though firmly in
the United Party camp, voted for his neighbouring
member Belo. Only five members of the PPP were
present to support the Government.

Then, contrary to normal practice, the House was
adjourned until 8 p.m. that evening to conclude the
issue and transact other business dealing with the further transfer of powers from the Australian Government to Papua New Guinea. The Opposition plan to
continue to frustrate the Government's intention was to
absent themselves from the evening meeting and to call
a quorum as soon as business was commenced. Parao
attended to perform this function and the tactic was
successful as the House failed to muster a quorum and
the meeting was automatically terminated. The ministerial motion remains on the notice paper for action at
the next meeting scheduled for 27 August.[10]

New Ministers after swearing-in. From left: Bruce Hephcott, John Kaputin, Les Johnson, Yano Belo, Pita Lus.

Finally the House approved the recommendations and the Minister for External Territories formally appointed Kaputin as Minister for Justice, Belo as Minister for Works and Lus to a rather curious combination of responsibilities, Police, Culture and Recreation. He looked the part when I swore him in.

The new Minister for Justice made haste to let everyone know where he stood. He arranged a public meeting to which he invited some two hundred guests to a dinner at the Papua Hotel — at government expense. There he delivered a long, wide-ranging speech, vilifying, not unjustly, many of the policies and practices of the colonial past.

The truth is that the law has been used throughout the years as an instrument of domination and oppression by the ruling classes. The law does not stand on neutral principles between men dispensing justice — it has created, consolidated and perpetuated class privileges — it has denied opportunities to certain groups of people — and it has heaped humiliation on the poor and the oppressed. We do not have to resort to any high flown academic theory to expose the true nature of law — certainly Papua New Guineans do not have to do this. We have been at the receiving end of the stick since the first white men reached the island.

In this country the law was an instrument of col- onialism and a means whereby the economic dom- inance of the white man was established over us. In other words the law was not a universal and abstract principle, it was specific and it made numerous distinc- tions between the white and the black. And not only did it deprive us of our land, but forced us to work for expatriate owners to whom the law gave our land. . . .

There is a danger that unless we take positive and affirmative steps, the colonial law will continue its stranglehold on our economic and social lives. Through its Eight-Point-Plan the Government is committed to a programme of radical change. It is my duty as Minister for Justice to ensure that the law does not obstruct the achievement of this programme. Indeed the law, as a weapon for social justice, must positively help to accelerate this major enterprise.[11]

Other events also marked 1973. The three arms of the defence forces were amalgamated under the overall command of the army commander, Brigadier Jim Norrie, in part as a preparation for handover to Papua New Guinea control on independence. The year also saw the death of two prominent members of the House of Assembly. During the September meeting of the House Matt Toliman, then Leader of the Opposition, suffered a heart attack and died. He had served in the House since 1964 and from that date until 1972 he had been a member of the Administrator's Council, an Under-Secretary in the first House and a Ministerial

Member in the second. He was liked and respected by both his allies and his political opponents. His body was taken into Parliament House after a requiem mass at Port Moresby Cathedral before it was flown to Rabaul where he was buried near his home village in the Gazelle Peninsula. Somare and I, with a number of prominent parliamentarians, flew to Rabaul to take part in an immense funeral, a tribute to a leader of the Tolai people. In November, Paulus Arek, the Minister for Information, and the Chairman of the second Select Committee for Constitutional Development, also died, after a long illness. His body, too, was brought into the House of Assembly for Members to pay their respects prior to an emotional funeral in Port Moresby.

There were two other notable departures during the year, but fortunately only to retirement in Australia — Tony Newman, Deputy Administrator, and Tom Ellis, Director of the Department of District Administration. Both were official members of the House of Assembly. Newman had been there, in the Legislative Council prior to 1964, and had served continuously in the House of Assembly. With their departure the number of official members in the House shrank to two, Bill Kearney, Secretary for Law, and Harry Ritchie, the Treasurer. Somare had wished to retain some official membership, in the first place for the professional advice they could offer the House and second because he could rely upon their support, something he could not always be assured of from his own supporters. Other than when their expertise was called upon, and when Australian Government interests were involved, official members, since 1972, had left the floor of the House to elected members. Papua New Guinea went into self-government with the colonial relic of some expatriate official membership still a part of the parliamentary system.

NOTES

1. First Interim Report of the Constitutional Planning Committee (Port Moresby, September 1973), PP.
2. Ibid., p. 32.
3. Ibid., p. 33.
4. P.N.G. news release, 22 May 1973, PP.
5. Speech by Dr Adam Malik, 13 November 1973, PP.
6. *The Economic Development of the Territory of Papua and New Guinea*, IBRD, John Hopkins Press, p. 35.
7. *Report on the Development Strategies for Papua New Guinea*, February 1973. It should be noted that the report was prepared before the advent of the Somare Government.
8. Ibid., p. 6.
9. P.N.G., House of Assembly, 1973.
10. Memorandum among PP.
11. Speech delivered 21 November 1973, PP.

15

ON THE BRINK

November 1973 saw us all in some haste to ensure that all the "t's" were crossed and the "i's" dotted to ensure a smooth transition. Morrison arrived in Papua New Guinea in mid-November with a large retinue from his Department to be confronted with a much larger group from the Papua New Guinea side. There were five Ministers and their advisers, five members of the Constitutional Planning Committee (CPC) and *their* advisers, plus the Leader of the Opposition and one other United Party member. I was there, and so too was Malcolm Lyon, representing the Australian Department of Foreign Affairs.

The meeting extended over 17 and 18 November but, in fact, did not cover any new ground. The CPC representatives, bolstered by the new Minister for Justice, Kaputin, bored us all to distraction on the subject of citizenship, and later on proposed policies the Committee believed the Australian Government should pursue in providing aid for a self-governing or independent Papua New Guinea. At the request of the CPC, Morrison agreed that in some areas, principally those relating to the administration of justice, final powers would be reserved for a later transfer. The Committee's rationale for this unusual request was that they were of such constitutional importance that, in each case, major provisions should be included in the Constitution itself and not be pre-empted by cosy agreements between the colonial government and the present, perhaps temporary Papua New Guinea government.

At the conclusion of the talks Tei Abal, leader of the Opposition, intervened with a measured warning from the conservatives. He said that the opposition held different views from those of the Government, and felt that transfer of powers was costing a great deal and taking place too rapidly. The United Party dissociated itself from the possible confusion of the future.[1]

The press release issuing from the Conference noted:

> As well as Defence and Foreign Relations, which are reserved in the *Papua New Guinea Act*, the Governor-General would be asked to proclaim matters dealing with the Papua New Guinea Supreme Court, the administration of courts, the Public Solicitor, prosecution, electoral policy and House of Assembly matters:
>
> > These matters were being proclaimed at the request of the CPC and will remain reserved until Papua New Guinea's Constitution becomes operative. . . .
> > Mr Morrison re-affirmed Australian policy which was that it would only act in the reserved areas after consulting with, and obtaining the advice of Papua New Guinea.[2]

Indeed this latter situation had pertained almost throughout 1973. To a very large extent Papua New Guinea was self-governing in fact, if not in name, prior to 1 December.

A matter of less importance to anyone but me was the future position of the Administrator whose principal function, according to Section 13 of the *Papua New Guinea Act*, would disappear; "There shall be an administrator of the Territory who shall be charged with the duty of administering the government of the Territory on behalf of the Commonwealth." Somare had already asked me to stay on but Whitlam had suggested that I should leave as soon as a self-governing Papua New Guinea had settled down and return to Australia to head up a new statutory body to administer Australia's foreign aid programme. My departure from Papua New Guinea would signal a new Australia/Papua New Guinea relationship with my replacement by a career diplomat and the formal establishment of an Australian High Commission. I thought myself that this was the best possible solution. In fact I knew too much about the inside story of the administration of the country, and had an uncomfortable knowledge of where the bodies were buried. I was happy to plan on going while I was still held in some esteem, and calculated on leaving in March or April 1974. Meanwhile my new role had to be defined and a suitable title found, and the latter problem seemed to exercise some Department of Foreign Affairs officials unduly. They appeared to have some apprehension that a title such as High Commissioner might give formal recognition to one they tended to think might become a cuckoo in their nest, and in any case inappropriate for one whose appointment, was not made formally by the Queen.

However, after some to-ing and fro-ing, an acceptable definition was achieved, and the appellation "High Commissioner" approved. Morrison wrote to the Australian Prime Minister seeking approval of the Prime Minister for the following role:

1. Head of State functions, in relation to appointments, legislation and ceremonials.
2. Executive functions on behalf of the Australian Government.
3. Senior government representation functions, e.g. to

exercise supervisory authority over all Australian departmental representatives in Papua New Guinea and also be the formal channel in Papua New Guinea for communication between the Australian and Papua New Guinea Governments.

Subsequently Whitlam wrote to me in the following terms:

> First you will know that the Government has decided that the title of Administrator of Papua New Guinea should, when Papua New Guinea becomes self-governing on 1st December 1973, be changed to that of High Commissioner. It is the wish of my Government and of Mr Somare that you should continue as High Commissioner at this time so that your great experience in Papua New Guinea affairs will be available to both governments at a period of considerable significance to Papua New Guinea and to the relations which are developing between that country and Australia. I would hope that you would be prepared to remain in this appointment until about March 1974 when, we hope, good progress will have been made in the drafting and presentation to the House of Assembly of a Constitution for Papua New Guinea.[3]

Pending that departure I was to be a somewhat hybrid animal.

The Constitutional Planning Committee also managed to get in its second Interim Report before self-government. It was a substantial document of some fifty pages containing thirty-three interim recommendations, a good many of them worthy expressions of intent rather than recipes for action; for instance Interim Recommendation 2: "The Constitution should incorporate the fundamental social goals of Papua New Guinea". Interim Recommendation 4: "Prominence should be given in the fundamental goals to the necessity that Papua New Guinea should make its own decisions and that its sovereignty should not be reduced by

external political, economic or military dependence;
that national leaders should always be free to make
national decisions. Papua New Guinea must avoid a
situation where foreign capital controls the destiny of
its people."[4] It was all a bit like an essay in praise of
motherhood.

Although the Committee had discussed citizenship
interminably there still appeared to be a long way to go
as the only recommendation relating to it was: "In principle citizens of Papua New Guinea should not be
allowed to hold concurrently the citizenship of another
country."

The report however did deal in more concrete terms
with the subject closest to the heart of some of its prominent members, notably Momis — that is, provincial
or district government. Fifteen of its recommendations
were devoted to this topic, most of them in quite
specific terms, though without touching on the central
issue of what powers provincial governments should
have. For example, Interim Recommendation 13: "The
provincial assemblies should consist of a minimum of
fifteen members with an additional member for every
10,000 people in the province in excess of 150,000."
And see Interim Recommendation 23: "Certain powers
should be vested by law in provincial governments."
Nor did the recommendations on the legislature touch
on the central issues of how political power should be
attained and distributed. The cart seemed to be a good
way in front of the horse.

There was general disappointment that so little
material progress had been made. It seemed that if an independence date had to await the completion of a final
Constitutional Report and its consideration by parliament before the final adoption of a Papua New Guinea
Constitution it might be delayed considerably beyond
Somare's projected date of September 1974.

The parliament of a non-self-governing Territory met for the last time over the period 12 to 27 November. Its main business was, of course, to approve the transfer of powers, which was accomplished with the grudging consent of the United Party. But most heat was generated by a Bill to increase the salaries of junior Ministers by $1000 p.a. to $7000, as Somare now planned that all Ministers should be Cabinet members, perhaps in emulation of the Australian Labor Party. Somare had sweetened the pot by a provision to increase similarly the emoluments of the Leader of the Opposition and his deputy. He was disappointed when that leader, Tei Abal, supported the latter provision but opposed the increase for Ministers. Ultimately a motion of censure on the issue was soundly rejected forty-six to twenty-eight. The parliamentary opposition had co-operated to ensure that self-government could come on 1 December, but gave fair warning that it would not be so compliant in the future. It would rigorously examine all proposals and insist on debating fully the measures put forward.

Also in November I compiled a despatch for the Minister for External Territories, my last as Administrator and his last in that specific Ministerial role. Some extracts follow:

Government and House of Assembly

The NCG continues to maintain a comfortable though fluctuating majority in the House of Assembly in the most important policy decisions. There remains the risk that on particular issues it may be defeated but in normal circumstances such defeat would not be regarded as a vote of no confidence in the Government. There are still rumours of the defection of the PPP, an event which at the present time seems unlikely though there is sign of a growing divergence in economic policy proposals between the PPP and the more radical members of the Cabinet. Even so, a PPP defection may not mean a loss of a majority for Somare, as he may be able to patch together sufficient uncommitted votes to stay in office. In my view, Tei Abal would be reluctant to upset the Government on other than a vital issue. One such issue in Abal's mind at present would be an early date for independence. However, I am confident that the Somare government will remain in office substantially unchanged.

Preparatory to formal self-government there has been a separation of the functions of Cabinet and the Executive Council. The Chief Minister now includes all twenty Ministers in Cabinet discussions, which does nothing to expedite the decision-making process but does add strength to what might be termed the radical wing of Cabinet as its members comprise the more vocal and opinionated Ministers. Many Ministers come to Cabinet meetings without having read the submissions or having had adequate briefing. This means that decisions reached are sometimes not based on the facts presented but rather on emotional responses to particular aspects of oral presentations. Some Ministers spend insufficient time on the business of their Ministries and are unduly preoccupied with the promotion of individual political designs and projects. The Chief Minister suffers from the present legal obstacles to removal of inefficient or embarrassing Ministers but although this difficulty will disappear when the amendments to the *Papua New Guinea Act* come into force on 1 December, it is unlikely that any Ministers will be dispossessed. The extent of shame suffered by a sacked Minister would be so great that any Melanesian would have very great hesitation in being the cause of it. Given all of these difficulties the business of government goes ahead and in general responsible decisions emerge.

The relationship between the Government and the House of Assembly remains rather tenuous. Members of Parliament devote a large part of their time to pursuing individual and parochial interests through the device of proposing resolutions or introducing matters

of public importance. Parliamentary subject committees do not work well and in some cases do not meet at
all. Party discipline is weak and because back benchers
are given little role by the Government in debate on
legislation there is a deal of frustration and erratic individual contributions to debate. The Opposition
suffers less from this than the Coalition as it can plan its
attacks and involve a majority of its numbers. The
Government tends to stick to Ministers to present its
case and Coalition supporters thus have little involvement. In a hundred-Member House it is quite impossible to give sufficient time to individual contributions
to debate without firm party discipline.

The House of Assembly influences Government
more through the existence of standing committees, if
the Chairman happens to be an activist, and also by the
creation of Select Committees. Persistent Chairmen
may become important factors in policy formulation.
There needs to be a full scale review of parliamentary
practices, procedures and organization. It may be that
the Constitutional Planning Committee will cause this
to be initiated. The trick is to have what might be called
participatory democracy as well as positive government
and the expeditious implementation of firm policies.

Self-government, independence and constitutional changes

The country as a whole appears to have accepted self-
government in a relaxed manner. The campaign conducted by all associated with Government policy,
though low key, was effective, but one reason for its
acceptance was the transfer of the opposition to self-
government to rejection of early independence. It may
be that independence can also be sold effectively but it
would be rash to press upon a particular date until there
has been a wide-spread consensus that a self-governing
Papua New Guinea is doing well. I expect that a date in
the second half of 1974 may become acceptable if there
are no unusual difficulties in the early part of the year.
Right now I think that it would be difficult to get a
parliamentary majority for a date earlier than 1975.
The principal fear is that early independence will

precipitate the departure of expatriates in greater numbers than is desirable and although in some ways this is a dependence syndrome it is also a recognition that there are as yet too few Papua New Guineans of sufficient training and experience to fill their places. The earlier apprehension that Australian financial aid would cease appears to have been relieved by repeated categorical assurances by responsible Australians.

Public Order

The situation has not changed much in the past several months. Urban crime remains at a high but not uncontrollable level. Large-scale urban disorder remains a threat and could erupt at any time over trivial issues but at present tensions are not high. Tribal fighting seems to be increasing and is presently arousing a belligerent vocal response from the Chief Minister, who promises tougher actions and stronger retributions. It is difficult to see this as being effective and indeed police violence may be met with organized counter-violence. The use of firearms by police may well be countered by shotguns in the hands of tribesmen, leading to an escalation of violence. I am alarmed that the Papua New Guinea government may feel itself obliged to make good its words with unpredictable results.

At present, deaths and injuries in tribal fighting are a good deal fewer than those caused by traffic accidents. Only traditional weapons are used and fighting still has something of the characteristics of a ritual, though with grim overtones. The measures taken by the police to control the warfare are ineffective and arrests and imprisonment of random tribesmen is not a deterrent. Wars are made by tribal leaders and it is these who should be punished for precipitating the conflicts. This means a sharp departure from existing practices in law but it is necessary if adequate control is to be exercised.

Overall the balance of power is not precarious but the general situation is volatile and it is a sensible precaution to ensure that adequate trained, disciplined forces are available to meet all eventualities. This means a defined role for the Defence forces in internal security, and training in conjunction with the Constabulary to meet that role.

The last words of this last despatch seem to form a suitable conclusion for this chapter.

It would be over-optimistic to say that the auguries for the future of Papua New Guinea were bright but certainly they are not bad. Papua New Guinea can look forward to financial aid which will enable the continuation of social and economic development at a far higher level than almost any other developing country. Not only this, but its own potentialities give rise to hope that it could have a viable economy without significant outside aid during the 1980s.

Its principal deficiency is its lack of trained manpower and its inexperienced leadership. In common with other developing countries it will continue to have a larger influx of people to the towns than its social services can cater for and greater than the available employment opportunities. It will continue to have young men and women dissatisfied with rural life and seeking, unavailingly, expanded opportunities to use knowledge and skills acquired in schools. It may react with an attempt to impose stronger restraints on movement and harsher law enforcement in towns. It will continue to have the problem of disorientation caused by the rapid changes in the Papua New Guinea society.

However, the Papua New Guinean is essentially a realist. He has already absorbed several lifetimes of changes in the past ten years and has learned to use not only the technology of the present decade but has also adapted its patterns of thought to his own use. Papua New Guinea is vigorous, forward-looking and confident; it has formidable difficulties in front of it but there is no reason to think that it cannot surmount them — though scrambling rather than soaring over them seems more likely.[5]

NOTES

1. Official record of discussion, PP.
2. Press release, 18 November 1973, PP.
3. Whitlam to Johnson, 23 September 1973, PP.
4. Second Interim Report of the Constitutional Planning Committee, November 1973, PP.
5. Administrator to Minister, External Territories, November 1973, PP.

16

SELF-GOVERNMENT DAY

"Self-government" may have been a bone of contention among the major political parties and a topic for earnest debate among the politically conscious segment of the population, but for the majority of Papua New Guineans it was a mysterious happening which might produce some unforeseen and perhaps alarming events. Indeed there was a possibility that there might be serious disturbances to mark the occasion.

There were a number of grounds to fear that there could be riots and a range of other unlawful acts. Despite an extensive public relations programme explaining the meaning of self-government and reassuring the people that it would mean no difference to their pattern of living, there was a good deal of uncertainty as to what to expect when the much debated but little understood "self-government" came about. Some expected that on that day they would take over all of the possessions of the white people, and some gave notice that they planned to do it by force. Others thought that it might be an opportunity to repay old scores and perhaps to regain land lost in earlier tribal affrays before the arrival of the white men froze the boundaries then existing. There was a possibility that separatist movements might seize the occasion to assert their claims to autonomy.

Planning to deal with these several eventualities proceeded on a number of different levels. The Papua New Guinea Cabinet decided that, as drink was the root of a good deal of evil, there should be a ban on the sale of alcohol over the weekend (1 December was a Saturday), and indeed tavern drunks were a source of potential affrays which could lead to large-scale tribal rioting. The Police Commissioner, in association with the Chief Minister and with me, disposed his riot squads in areas of possible conflagration — the Western Highlands and Chimbu, Port Moresby, Rabaul and Kieta — while we dusted off the formal requirements to request Defence Force assistance should the position get beyond the control of the police. The Executive Council Security Committee (Somare, Guise, Kavali, Chan, Kiki and I), authorized the preparation of an order invoking appropriate clauses of the Public Order Ordinance should its use prove necessary. No public celebrations were arranged so as to prevent the congregation of excited, volatile crowds. There was concern that a meeting arranged by the Papua Besena movement for 1 December might provide a spark for the Port Moresby powder barrel.

In the event, self-government weekend was the most quiet and trouble free of the year. The only official ceremony to mark the occasion was conducted in the studio of the Department of Information at 10 a.m. on Saturday 1 December 1973. There, in front of a small gathering of invited guests and a formidable group of cameramen, the Chief Justice, John Minogue, swore me in as High Commissioner of Papua New Guinea, and I, in turn, administered the Executive Council oath of secrecy to the Chief Minister and six of his colleagues (Messrs Mola, Kavali, Okuk, Lapun, Kiki and Taureka), who took oaths in English and Pidgin.

I made a brief speech:

> We are fortunate to be here on one such occasion when
> Michael Somare makes his mark as the leader of his
> people, on the day that Papua New Guinea becomes
> self-governing. There will be other marks to be made
> — on Constitution Day and Independence Day — and
> these may be greater occasions, but today Papua New
> Guinea begins to make its way from the colonial womb
> to independent nationhood. Chief Minister, you bear

Self-Government Day, 1 December 1973; Michael Somare takes the oath.

the hopes — and the fears — of all of your people. May
the fears be banished and the hopes realized.[1]

and Somare responded in kind: "My government and
my people take up our responsibility with confidence."

The newly-constituted Executive Council then met
formally for five minutes and then recessed to join the
guests for some self-government refreshments. The
whole thing took less than thirty minutes.

The only shadow remaining was the possible out-
come of the Papua Besena march and the rally to
culminate in a Papua Besena flag raising at Kila Kila, a
suburb of Port Moresby at about 11 a.m. I drove out
there myself after the ceremony and found a substantial
crowd of people there and a good humoured group of
marchers approaching the rallying point. There was no
apparent tension and the meeting, involving a thousand
or so participants and spectators, passed off without
incident.

That evening, probably in common with many other
centres, we had a big and cheerful party in the garden
of Government House during which the Chief Minister,
by this time in a rather exhilarated mood, made a fine
speech which everyone cheered but of which nobody
took a record. Also during the evening I presented the
George medal to Patrick Tau Gau, one of the few survivors of the tragic Caribou air crash which killed
almost all of the cadet passengers. Patrick's award was
for heroism in rescuing some of his fellows from the
crash and in sustaining them until help arrived.

Australian and other foreign media representatives,
in Papua New Guinea for the occasion, recorded self-
government in Papua New Guinea as the non-event of
the year, and many of these worthy souls were openly
disgruntled at the absence of something spectacular in
the way of mayhem, murder or riot; which causes one

Self-Government evening. From left: Michael Somare, Les Johnson, Dulcie Johnson.

to reflect on the standards of journalism imposed on the community by the media, or perhaps on the known predilections of the community imposed on the media.

The Australian parliament had already conveyed to the Papua New Guinea House of Assembly its congratulations and warm wishes on the occasion of Papua New Guinea's achievement of self-government. Bill Morrison moved the motion which was seconded by the previous Minister for External Territories, Andrew Peacock. Each claimed his Party's prime responsibility for the successful conclusion of Papua New Guinea's passage to self-government.

Morrison claimed: "Less than four years ago the then

Australian Government regarded self-government and independence as a remote possibility. The visits of 1970 and 1971 of the then leader of the opposition, the present Prime Minister (Mr Whitlam) broke the nexus. His proposal for early self-government and independence was met with official hostility and public dismay. But the course and flow of events were dramatically and irrevocably changed."

Peacock responded: "This is not the occasion to express party political differences. The orderly and peaceful transition of Papua New Guinea to self-government . . . may be regarded to a large extent as a tribute to the policies of the previous Liberal/Country Party government. The date was agreed upon last year by the Liberal/Country Party Government of Australia and the Government of Papua New Guinea."

I guess they were both right.

Perhaps as a postscript to the occasion it is as well to record the satisfaction expressed in the United Nations at this transition of one of its colonial charges. At the General Assembly of December 1973 the Fourth Committee adopted one of the customarily wordy resolutions when, among other "welcomes" "calls upon", "reaffirms", "takes note of", "requests" it.

> *Emphasizes* the imperative need to ensure that the national unity of Papua New Guinea is preserved.
> *Strongly endorses* the policies of the administering power and of the Government of Papua New Guinea aimed at discouraging separatist movements, and at promoting national unity.
> *Stresses* the right of the people of Papua New Guinea to control and dispose of their natural resources in their national interest.
> *Stresses also* the importance of preserving the cultural heritage of the people of Papua New Guinea.[2]

From my point of view it was almost all over as far as

direct responsibility for Papua New Guinea affairs was concerned. For the past year my role had been contracting. Of Australia's two remaining responsibilities, defence and foreign affairs, the latter had already effectively passed into Papua New Guinea hands. The Australian position was set out in a memo to me from the Department of Foreign Affairs.

> While the Australian Government will wish to maintain its formal position on the reservation of the foreign affairs power until independence it will expect and indeed encourage the Government of Papua New Guinea and the Minister for Defence and Foreign Relations and his department to exercise an increasing independence on the formation and conduct of Papua New Guinea foreign relations, subject of course to consultation with Australia in important policy matters.[3]

I was the formal channel of communication between the two parties, a responsibility which did not occupy too much of my time.

The Australian Department of Defence was less ready to relinquish its responsibilities for it had a great deal more to give up. The Papua New Guinea Defence Force was still an Australian unit. It was commanded by an Australian Brigadier and Australian officers and NCOs were still members of the Pacific Islands Regiment. Australian defence strategy still involved the use of the PIR and of bases within Papua New Guinea. The transfer of responsibility to the Papua New Guinea government had to be a much more careful and precise process. Its accomplishment post-dated these memoirs. Defence matters were never ones in which I was encouraged to meddle and defence communications went directly to the Defence Force Commander, a circumstance which my predecessors and I found irksome.

While preparations for self-government were proceeding an Australian office had been established in

Port Moresby as the genesis of an Australian High Commission. It was staffed largely by Foreign Affairs officers and admirably managed by Malcolm Lyon of that department. The office was located in an office block originally established for the Commonwealth Department of Works, now phased out of activities in Papua New Guinea. The building was not too far from my office so that I could manage some surveillance of its activities without too much physical disturbance.

Defence activities were centred on Murray Barracks five or six kilometres from the town centre. The Commander was scrupulous in briefing me regularly on the affairs of the force. I was happy to see that the Papua New Guinea heir apparent to the Australian Commander was Ted Diro. I had known him, and his wife, since they were at school.

As my executive functions were sharply reduced I had to resist temptation to pry into matters which were no longer my concern and I began to find time rather heavy on my hands. Somare had previously asked me to say until independence but the arrangement I had made with Whitlam and the obvious eagerness of the Department of Foreign Affairs to get its man into Papua New Guinea ruled out acceptance of the invitation.

The last days of my tenure of office were enlivened by the visit of the Queen, accompanied by Prince Philip and the honeymooners Princess Anne and Captain Phillips. Lord Mountbatten was also in the party. In the space of five rather hectic days they visited Bougainville, Rabaul, Goroka, Lae and Port Moresby and were warmly received everywhere. We found them pleasant and easy-going guests, though playing host to the Queen does have its protocol anxieties. The visit encouraged local debate as to whether an independent Papua New Guinea would opt to be a republic or a

The Queen's arrival in Bougainville 1974. From left: Prince Philip, Veronica Somare, the Queen, Michael Somare and Paul Lapun, the senior Bougainville politician and Minister for Mines.

Prince Philip accompanied by the Chancellor, Sir John Crawford, gets a traditional welcome at the University of Papua New Guinea.

monarchy. I think that the visit may have done a good deal to sway opinion towards the monarchical solution, and, no doubt, delighted the recipients of the spate of imperial honours which accompanied the independence celebrations in September 1975. Veronica and Michael Somare and my wife and I accompanied the royal party from Bougainville to Rabaul on the "Britannia", during which Somare was charmed by the Queen and left the ship a firm royalist.

My wife and I left Papua New Guinea in March 1974 after more than twelve years there. We regard it as the most interesting and fulfilling years of our lives. We feel fortunate indeed to have had a part to play in the transition of Papua New Guinea from a neglected colonial Territory to a vigorous independent nation.

NOTES

1. PN.G. press release, December 1973, PP.
2. Transcript from Australian Mission to the United Nations, December 1973, PP.
3. Memo, Foreign Affairs to Administrator, 5 September 1973, PP.

17

EPILOGUE

The long period of Australian intervention in the affairs of Papua New Guineans effectively ceased on 1 December 1973, though total legal separation was still twenty-one months away. Thereafter Australia was one among a number of foreign powers with interests in the country. But Australian influence would continue to overshadow the attitudes and decisions of Papua New Guineans. The maintenance of a viable State would be dependent on the continuation of massive Australian grants. Personal relationships established between individual Australians and Papua New Guineans would ensure a level of exchange not usual between foreign powers. Australian farmers and businessmen resident in the country would still be a strong, even dominant, influence on the Papua New Guinea economy. Many would become naturalized citizens and some would continue to be members of Parliament, even to have Ministerial office. Australian schools, universities and other training institutions would harbour Papua New Guineans. The help and advice of Australian experts would continue to be sought.

For better or for worse the Papua New Guinean State was an Australian creation. Its system of government, its administration services, its defence force, its economy were all essentially Australian in nature. The model for the establishment of government in Papua New Guinea was derived from our own colonial heritage. We began by establishing Legislative Councils which were entirely advisory in character. In Papua the first Council was set up in 1905 with six official and three nominated non-officials — of course all expatriate. In 1933 New Guinea, a mandated Territory, had its first Council. There were fifteen members, seven of whom were nominated non-officials, again all expatriates.

When the administrations of Papua and New Guinea were united after World War II we had to start all over again with a Legislative Council presided over by the Administrator and having twenty-eight other members, sixteen of them nominated officials, three elected non-official expatriates, three non-officials representing the Christian Missions, also expatriates, three other nominated non-official expatriates and three nominated Papua New Guineans. It goes without saying that all expatriates had to be of British nationality. The foundations of a ministry were also established in an Executive Council which somewhat undemocratically consisted of the Administrator and nine nominated public servants. This quasi-Government machine met for the first time in November 1951.

Reform, or perhaps evolution, had to wait for nine years, when the Administration surrendered its official majority in the Legislative Council and Papua New Guinea representation, though still nominal, became more substantial. Of a Council of thirty-seven, (including the Administrator as Chairman) there were six Papua New Guineans elected via an electoral college system and five other nominated indigenes. The Executive Council, renamed the Administrator's Council, also included three elected members of the Legislative Council of which at least one was required to be Papua New Guinean. We were moving steadily down the path, taken by ex-British colonies, towards an elected parliament.

From here we took the plunge which, in 1964, produced the first House of Assembly, with members elected in single member constituencies by universal franchise, though ten electorates were reserved for expatriates and there were still ten appointed officials. In all this first real parliament comprised sixty-four members, of whom sixteen were elected expatriates (six of them won non-reserved seats), ten expatriate officials and thirty-eight elected Papua New Guineans. At the same time the Administrator's Council was democratized. It was now to comprise the Administrator as Chairman, three officials and seven elected members of the House of Assembly, five of them indigenes. Thus the Council was nicely balanced — five expatriates, five Papua New Guineans, with an expatriate Chairman. However the Council never achieved more than an advisory role. The horse was not likely to bolt with the rider and, in fact, never made any serious attempt to do so.

The first House of Assembly established the Westminster pattern. Its procedures and its rituals were similar, its Standing Orders were modelled on the Commonwealth parliament, and its reference was May's *Parliamentary Practices*. The Speaker and his clerks wore wigs and gowns.

There was, of course, debate as to Papua New Guinea's political future and consideration of the alternatives to a straight Westminster–type democracy. John Guise startled our Canberra colleagues by introducing a motion in the House of assembly to set up a Select Committee on Constitutional Development, and we members of that Committee examined the constitutions of a number of developing countries looking for suitable, if composite, models. We thought about the broad alternatives. Should we have an all-powerful parliament, from which was drawn the executive government, or an all-powerful Head of State with parliament an advisory body only, or a balance of powers between an elected parliament and a President? We automatically assumed that the judiciary would keep the parties honest.

We already had, in fact, a little of each. The Minister for External Territories through the person of the Administrator was an all-powerful figure though he did have an elected Papua New Guinea parliament which could legislate on whatever matters it cared to, though the Administrator, either himself or through an Australian Governor-General, could veto such legislation. There was a written Constitution (the *Papua New Guinea Act*), which could be interpreted by the High Court of Australia. But between 1965 and 1967 when the Select Committee was deliberating we were not far enough down the road towards self-determination to propose radical changes in the nature of government, and if we had they were unlikely to be acceptable to the colonial power, Australia.

The second Constitutional Committee established in 1969 did likewise. We found it difficult to break what was now an established mould. Neither the members of the Committee nor Papua New Guineans at large had any alternative experience on which to draw, nor, indeed, any indigenous institutions which could conceivably be a base for new beginnings. Papua New Guinea was a collection of small fragmented communities, there was no system of chieftainship (except in the Trobriand Islands), no organized decision-making processes, other than by lengthy discussion in an attempt to arrive at a consensus, no dominant tribal group, no permanent alliances between groups, and no sense of nationality. There was no organized labour movement and no political parties drawing widespread support, though the innovative Tony Voutas made a try at establishing a nation-wide party based on local government councils. Inevitably we could see no further than the development of the existing institution. It should be said that the exhaustive deliberations of the Constitutional Planning Committee set up by the Somare Government could not come up with anything better.

I do not believe that the Australian Government should be open to criticism because of the imposition of a parliamentary government in the Australian image, though it was not quite in that image, because the second Constitutional Committee resisted the suggestion of the Minister for External Territories that an upper House should be established to review the activities of the lower. We settled for a unicameral system. In the House itself, however, the wisdom of the adoption of Australian parliamentary procedures was certainly open to question. It inhibited the participation of many members in the affairs of the nation but enhanced the dominance of the executive government, whether it be that of the colonial power or the indigenous government. In the early days of the House of Assembly we needed many more advisory staff and much more time devoted to the matters listed for parliamentary resolution. Of course revised practices may have made the task of the Administration much more difficult and possibly it may have led to serious challenges to policy but it would have developed a stronger indigenous political base for an independent country.

Another criticism that could be directed at us was our

failure, in the sixties, to make a serious attempt to enhance the status of those Papua New Guineans who showed leadership potential and exercised some influence on their fellows. But given the go slow attitude towards political development by the Australian Government and the marked lack of desire among Administration officials to set up indigenous rivals to their status and authority we were content to let sleeping leaders lie. On the same front we discouraged the development of political parties which might challenge the authority of the Administration; not that there was a great deal of local impetus for political organization. Such as it was invariably came from expatriates. Parties germinated but did not flourish because of lack of Papua New Guinean interest. There were plenty of things about which Papua New Guineans could get steamed up but there was not sufficient contact between those who were affronted by such things as disparity of incomes, unequal opportunity, racial prejudice and so on. Papua New Guineans had been thoroughly brainwashed to accept their inferior status as the natural order of things. It was not until the development of tertiary education and training institutions that there was a forum for the expression of discontent. It was from this source that the first real indigenous political movements began. Even then the general opinion, both in the Papua New Guinea Administration and in Australian Government circles, was that the Pangu Pati was a disturbing radical factor in a well-ordered society. The alliance between the Administration and the conservative highlanders was used to beat down even quite modest initiatives from the Pangu members in the House of Assembly.

In the end we shed our colonial burden with almost indecent haste. It could be claimed that it was too hasty to ensure reasonable stability in our ex-colony. There are, of course, sound arguments for a measured, step-by-step process towards independence so that each movement is consolidated before proceeding to the next, but when can it be judged that a country is "ready" to run its own affairs? In fact Papua New Guinea had few of the requisites for independence. Its economy was largely in expatriate hands, it was almost entirely dependent on external financial aid to remain viable, its senior public servants were mostly expatriates, less than twenty per cent of its populace was literate; But it did have the one essential element for independence — a small but determined group of Papua New Guineans with the will to run their own affairs. Once such a body exists the game is over as soon as they become organized. Only stern repressive measures can delay it. Whatever attitude the Australian Government may have taken to the development of an independence movement the visit of Gough Whitlam in 1969/70 precluded any position but compliance with the wishes of the Papua New Guinea people as expressed through the House of Assembly.

Even so we made a rather headlong abdication. It was precipitated by the surprise advent of a Pangu Pati-led coalition dedicated to early self-government, but cautious about an independence timetable, and then further hastened by the victory of the Labor Party in Australia later in the same year, with that new Australian Government determined to shuck off its colonial image at the earliest possible date. Effective Australian influence ceased towards the end of 1973 when all Papua New Guinea requests for the transfer of powers had been granted. At this time, and subsequently too, the House of Assembly was a cluster of individuals with limited concepts of the responsibilities of a national parliament and with fluctuating loyalties towards their political leaders, often influenced by what favours might accrue to them. A couple of years of the exercise of restricted powers to gain experience in making choices and to enable the consolidation of political parties would certainly have ensured greater stability, but it could not be said that Papua New Guinea has done badly. In that sense Australia has some cause to feel satisfaction.

INDEX